Everyone Here Spoke Sign Language

Nora Ellen Groce

• • • • • • • • • • • • • • •

Everyone Here Spoke Sign Language

Hereditary Deafness on Martha's Vineyard

Harvard University Press
Cambridge, Massachusetts
and London, England

Library of Congress Cataloging in Publication Data
Groce, Nora, 1952–
    Everyone here spoke sign language.
    Bibliography: p.
    Includes index.
    1. Deaf—Massachusetts—Martha's Vineyard—History.
2. Deafness—Genetic aspects. 3. Sign language.
I. Title.
HV2561.M49G76 1985   362.4'2'0974494   85-5451
ISBN 0-674-27041-X (paper)

For E. Gale Huntington
  of Chilmark, Martha's Vineyard

•   •   •   •   •   •   •   •   •   •   •   •   •   •   •   •

Foreword

by John W. M. Whiting

This book is about Martha's Vineyard Island—especially the towns of West Tisbury and Chilmark—which for over two hundred years had a high incidence of hereditary deafness. The residents compensated for this condition by inventing or borrowing an efficient sign language, which was used by almost everyone, hearing and deaf alike. Although the last hereditary deaf person in Chilmark died in 1952, some of the older residents still remember the days when everyone spoke sign language. From the memories of these informants and a wealth of archival material, Nora Groce has compiled a detailed, vivid description of daily life on the Vineyard in the early days of this century. She shows the extraordinary degree to which deaf people were integrated into the community, for Vineyarders did not consider deafness to be a handicap.

Curiously enough, both the high incidence of deafness and the adoption of sign language resulted from marriage patterns brought by the original settlers when they emigrated in the seventeenth century from the English county of Kent. There, in the era before industrialization and urbanization, most people lived in communities of some ten or twelve families that remained in the same place for many generations. If they did move, they migrated as a group. In about 10 percent of the preindustrial societies whose marriage patterns are known, marriage within the community was preferred—a situation anthropologists call an endogamous deme. A child in such a community would grow up with all four grandparents and their families nearby. This leads to a highly supportive social network but also to a high degree of inbreeding. Groce provides historical evidence that the endogamous deme, common in rural England, was specifically reported for the area of Kent called the Weald, where the families here described originated.

In a small town such as Chilmark—as in the Weald—it took only a few generations for everyone to be related. Groce argues convincingly that more than one of the original Vineyard settlers carried a recessive gene for deafness, and the increasing interrelatedness of the Chilmark families over time made it ever more likely that the trait for deafness would be expressed in the population.

Because Mendel's theory of heredity was not widely known or accepted until after 1900, over the years numerous reasons for Vineyard deafness were put forward: the will of God, the sins of the father, fright during pregnancy. Alexander Graham Bell, who visited the Island and wrote several papers on it, thought the deafness might be caused by the layer of clay under the soil of Chilmark but not of the other towns on the Vineyard, where deafness was less common.

I was born in Chilmark and am related through my mother to most of the families in that community, which was essentially a huge extended family. Like any family, it had its rivalries and tensions, but it was unparalleled as a support group. I never learned to sign, but I saw sign language used when we went to the annual county fair at West Tisbury and when I went fishing out of Menemsha. Knowing how to use sign language was, like knowing French, something to be envied. With the influx of new residents from off-Island in this century, the incidence of hereditary deafness on the Vineyard declined and finally ceased altogether. But this benefit was countered by the destruction of the microcommunity as a strongly supportive network, something that is sadly missing in our modern industrial world.

• • • • • • • • • • • • • • •

Acknowledgments

I am indebted to a large number of people and organizations, many more than I can properly thank here. This research would not have begun without an initial suggestion and continual guidance from E. Gale Huntington, editor emeritus of the *Dukes County Intelligencer*. Gale and his wife, Mildred Tilton Huntington, took me into their home during my stays on the Vineyard and always made me feel welcome. They helped me make contacts on the Island, and no doubt many Islanders made time to talk to me because I was their friend. I am deeply indebted to both Gale and Mil.

The staff of the Dukes County Historical Society in Edgartown were unfailingly helpful and regularly went out of their way to provide information pertinent to my research. In particular, Arthur Railton, the current editor of the *Intelligencer*; Doris Stoddard, president; and Muriel Crossman, former secretary and librarian, were of invaluable assistance.

I am indebted to professors Lucile Newman, Robert Jay, and William Beeman of Brown University and to Pertti Pelto of the University of Connecticut for advice and guidance during the course of my research and for their careful reading of an earlier version of this manuscript. I am also grateful to Walter Nance of the Medical College of Virginia at Richmond, who most kindly allowed me access to his data on the nineteenth-century American deaf population. Peter Dunkley of the British Broadcasting Corporation directed my attention to Samuel Pepys's reference to sign language.

The staff of the Alexander Graham Bell Association for the Deaf in

Washington, D.C., deserve thanks, particularly Sarah Colon, director, and Salome Swaim, then a librarian at the John Hitz Memorial Library, who located Bell's notes on deafness.

Several historians in southeastern Massachusetts helped me trace the ancestry of deaf Vineyarders back through the seventeenth century. I gratefully acknowledge the assistance of Mertie E. Romaine of the Middleboro Historical Society, Russell A. Lovell, Jr., of the Sandwich Historical Society, and Channing E. Hoxie, town clerk of Sandwich, who located several photographs and poems. Charlotte Price of the Falmouth Historical Society deserves special thanks for regularly sending me information and answering my requests for help.

My research is based in large measure on oral history, and I am particularly indebted to all the Vineyarders who willingly shared their memories with me. I cannot thank individually all the Vineyarders who patiently answered my questions, looked up information, or gave me directions when I got lost on Island back roads. But I would like to express my thanks here to the following Vineyarders, who took the time to talk at length about the world they once knew: Joe Allen, Mike Athearn, Eva Benson, Norman Benson, Everel Black, John Black, Jerome Bruno, Eric Cottle, Gladys Flanders, Hazel Flanders, Doris Gifford, Willis Gifford, Mildred Hammett, Henry Beetle Hough, Fanny Jenkinson, Ida Karl, Stanton Lair, Mabel Look, George Magnuson, Anna Maxson, Esther Mayhew, Iva Mitchell, Colson Mitchell, Mary Morgan, Jeffrey Norton, Ernestine Peckham, Emily Poole, Donald Poole, Dorothy Cottle Poole, Lemuel Reed, Dionis Coffin Riggs, Emily Huntington Rose, Grover Ryan, Bertha Tilton Salvador, Hollis Smith, Alton Tilton, Laura Tilton, Thomas Tilton, Leonard Vanderhoop, Everett Whiting, John Whiting, and Ethel Whidden.

This work would not have been possible without a fellowship from the National Institute of Mental Health (Grant no. 5 F31 MH08262). Peg Anderson of Harvard University Press deserves special mention for helping me transform my manuscript into book form. I want to acknowledge the continuing encouragement I have received from my parents, Raymond and Marian Groce. Most especially, I would like to thank my husband, Lawrence Kaplan, who helped and encouraged me from the very beginning of my research, and my son Josiah.

Nora E. Groce
Cambridge, Massachusetts

Contents

Everyone Here Spoke Sign Language

• • • • • • • • • • • • • • •

"They Were Just Like Everyone Else"

One of Gale Huntington's favorite activities is driving his guests around the island of Martha's Vineyard, Massachusetts, at speeds never exceeding thirty-five miles an hour, and pointing out spots of historical interest. Gale's memory of the region goes back over eighty years, when coasting vessels crowded Vineyard Haven harbor and whale ships were still seen in New Bedford. He knows as much about the Island as anyone alive today. In the course of one of these jaunts "up-Island," in late October 1978, Gale pointed out Jedidiah's house to me.[1] "He was a good neighbor," said Gale, "He used to fish and farm some. He was one of the best dory men on the Island, and that was pretty good, considering he had only one hand."

"What happened to the other one?" I asked.

"Lost it in a mowing machine accident when he was a teenager." As an afterthought, he added, "He was deaf and dumb too."[2]

"Because of the accident?" I asked.

"Oh no," said Gale, "he was born that way."

On the way back to Vineyard Haven, as we puttered down a sandy ridge overlooking a wide expanse of Vineyard Sound, Gale glanced at a weatherbeaten clapboard house on the left and said, "Jedidiah's brother lived there." Nathaniel had owned a large dairy farm. "And," said Gale, putting his foot on the brakes by way of emphasis, "he was considered a very wealthy man—at least by Chilmark standards. Come to think of it, he was deaf and dumb too."

I wondered aloud why both brothers had been born deaf. Gale said no one had ever known why; perhaps the deafness was inherited. I suggested that it might have been caused by disease. But Gale didn't think so, because there were so many deaf people up-Island, and they were all related. There had been deaf Vineyarders as long as anyone could remember. The last one died in the early 1950s.

"How many deaf people were there?" I asked.

"Oh," said Gale, "I can remember six right offhand, no, seven."

"How many people lived in town here then?"

"Maybe two hundred," Gale replied, "maybe two hundred fifty. Not more than that."

I remarked that that seemed to be a very large number of deaf people in such a small community. Gale seemed surprised but added that he too had occasionally been struck by the fact that there were so many deaf people. No one else in town had treated this as unusual, however, so he had thought little more about it.

One rainy afternoon on my next trip to Martha's Vineyard, I sat down with Gale and tried to figure out the genealogies of the deaf Islanders whom he remembered. I thought that the deafness up-Island might have been the result of an inherited trait for deafness, and I wanted to do some research on the topic.

Gale's knowledge of Island history and genealogy was extensive. He sat in his living room smoking a few of those cigarettes expressly forbidden by his doctor and taking more than a few sips of his favorite New England rum as he reminisced about times long past and friends who had been dead half a century or more. As we talked, he recalled from his childhood three or four additional deaf people. When he was a boy in the early 1900s, ten deaf people lived in the town of Chilmark alone.

I had already spent a good part of the afternoon copying down various genealogies before I thought to ask Gale what the hearing people in town had thought of the deaf people.

"Oh," he said, "they didn't think anything about them, they were just like everyone else."

"But how did people communicate with them—by writing everything down?"

"No," said Gale, surprised that I should ask such an obvious question. "You see, everyone here spoke sign language."

"You mean the deaf people's families and such?" I inquired.

"Sure," Gale replied, as he wandered into the kitchen to refill his glass and find some more matches, "and everybody else in town too— I used to speak it, my mother did, everybody."

• Anthropology and the Disabled

Hereditary disorders in relatively isolated communities have long been known, and geneticists and physical anthropologists have studied a number of examples of recessive deafness in small communities.[3] Martha's Vineyard is one more such case. For over two and a half centuries the population of this island had a strikingly high incidence of hereditary deafness. In the nineteenth century, and presumably earlier, one American in every 5,728 was born deaf, but on the Vineyard the figure was one in every 155.[4] In all, I have identified at least seventy-two deaf persons born to Island families over the course of three centuries. At least a dozen more were born to descendants of Vineyarders who had moved off-Island.

In this book I draw on genetics, deaf studies, sociolinguistics, ethnography, and oral and written history to construct an ethnohistory of a genetic disorder. The complex mathematical models are more appropriate for medical genetic and physical anthropology journals and thus will be published elsewhere. Here I concentrate on the history of this genetic trait and on the history of the people who carried it, for the two are inseparable. A genetic disorder does not occur in a vacuum, somehow removed from the lives of the human beings affected by it. How do the affected people function within their society, and how do they perceive their own role in the community?

Traditionally, disabilities have been analyzed primarily in medical terms or, by social scientists, in terms of deviance. In the social science literature, deviance is defined as an attribute that sets the individual apart from the majority of the population, who are assumed to be normal.[5] Deafness is considered one of the most severe and widespread of the major disabilities.[6] In the United States alone, 14.2 million people have some hearing impairment that is severe enough to interfere with their ability to communicate; of these, 2 million are considered deaf (National Center for Health Statistics 1982).

A deaf person's greatest problem is not simply that he or she cannot hear but that the lack of hearing is socially isolating. The deaf person's knowledge and awareness of the larger society are limited because hearing people find it difficult or impossible to communicate with him or her. Even if the deaf person knows sign language, only a very small percentage of the hearing population can speak it and can communicate easily with deaf people. The difficulty in communicating, along with the ignorance and misinformation about deafness that is pervasive in most of the hearing world, combine to cause difficulties in all aspects of life for deaf individuals—in education, employment, community involvement, and civil rights.

On the Vineyard, however, the hearing people were bilingual in English and the Island sign language. This adaptation had more than linguistic significance, for it eliminated the wall that separates most deaf people from the rest of society. How well can deaf people integrate themselves into the community if no communication barriers exist and if everyone is familiar and comfortable with deafness? The evidence from the Island indicates that they are extremely successful at this.

One of the strongest indications that the deaf were completely integrated into all aspects of society is that in all the interviews I conducted, deaf Islanders were never thought of or referred to as a group or as "the deaf." Every one of the deaf people who is remembered today is thought of as a unique individual.[7] When I inquired about "the deaf" or asked informants to list all the deaf people they had known, most could remember only one or two, although many of them had known more than that. I was able to elicit comments about specific individuals only by reading informants a list of all the deaf people known to have lived on the Island. My notes show a good example of this when, in an interview with a woman who is now in her early nineties, I asked, "Do you know anything similar about Isaiah and David?"

"Oh yes!" she replied. "They both were very good fishermen, very good indeed."

"Weren't they both deaf?" I prodded.

"Yes, come to think of it, I guess they both were," she replied. "I'd forgotten about that."

On the mainland profound deafness is regarded as a true handicap, but I suggest that a handicap is defined by the community in which it appears. Although we can categorize the deaf Vineyarders as disabled, they certainly were not considered to be handicapped. They participated freely in all aspects of life in this Yankee community. They grew up, married, raised their families, and earned their livings in just the same manner as did their hearing relatives, friends, and neighbors. As one older man on the Island remarked, "I didn't think about the deaf any more than you'd think about anybody with a different voice."

Perhaps the best description of the status of deaf individuals on the Vineyard was given to me by an island woman in her eighties, when I asked about those who were handicapped by deafness when she was a girl. "Oh," she said emphatically, "those people weren't handicapped. They were just deaf."

• Sources

Because I have taken an ethnohistorical approach to a phenomenon that has usually been consigned to the field of medical genetics, it is important to explain how I gathered my information over the course of four years. After my initial discussion about deafness with Gale Huntington and his wife, I reviewed what had been published on deafness on the Island. Except for one or two articles in local newspapers from the nineteenth century and a handful of scattered references in nineteenth-century publications for the deaf, nothing had been written on this subject.

Written Records I then searched the available published and unpublished records concerning the Island for information about deaf residents. Vineyard records are unusually complete, but only in one or two instances did any of these records note that a person was deaf. With the exception of the federal census, which began to keep records on the number of deaf Americans in 1830, there was no place, and no need, to mention an individual's deafness on birth, marriage, or death records, land deeds, or tax accounts.[8]

Oral History Although it seemed that the lack of written information would limit my study of Vineyard deafness, I decided to gather as much from the records as possible. After several expeditions to the Island, I found that one source of informaton—oral history—was consistently useful. The oral historical tradition on Martha's Vineyard is remarkably strong, largely because the same families lived on the

Island for three centuries with very little dislocation. It was not unusual to interview an elderly Islander living in the house where his grandmother or great-grandmother had been born. Families stayed in the same small Island villages and hamlets for two or three centuries. Because of this continuity, the local traditions remained intact, and personalities and events had an immediacy and a contextual framework that would be unusual in a more fluid population.

No individuals with the inherited form of deafness that existed for several centuries on the Island are still alive. To find out about these people, I tried to interview every Vineyarder old enough to remember some of the Island deaf—neighbors, friends, relatives, people who had fished with deaf persons or attended church with them or could recall seeing them at the town meeting or the county fair. I paid particular attention to those people, mostly in their eighties and nineties, who remembered the deaf residents as active members of the community.[9] In all, I interviewed more than two hundred Islanders, including some who had moved off-Island. I spent the most time with a core group of about fifty people, all Island elders, whose vast knowledge of Vineyard people and events formed the basis of my research.[10] I was able to substantiate much of their oral tradition with written documents, and I have attempted to place it within a theoretical framework; but without the assistance of these Islanders, this book would be little more than a listing of names and dates.

Historians, oral historians, and folklorists have long argued over the relative merits of oral and written records. I tried to anticipate and compensate for many of the potential problems by cross-checking oral and written sources against each other. (For a more detailed discussion of this subject and of some problems I encountered, see Appendix A.)

Only two of the older Islanders declined to be interviewed. At first, however, many people claimed they did not know enough to be helpful. Most informants regarded what they remembered as private memories, family anecdotes, and local gossip; they were intrigued to find that their memories tied in with dozens of other recollections. Often, if I mentioned a name, an informant would say, "Why, I haven't thought of him in years." If I mentioned an event that another Islander had told me about, the person would ask, "Where did you ever hear about that? I didn't think anyone else remembered."

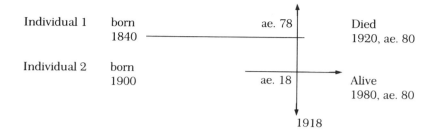

Islanders are acutely aware and justifiably proud of their past. Elderly residents, remembering stories their parents and grandparents told them, created a chain of memories extending back to about 1850, a span of 130 years. The most recent events were more clearly in focus, but the older Islanders were familiar with names, dates, and stories, back to 1850 and were able to place individuals in a social matrix. This time span seems to form the limit on active oral history. A man who was eighty in 1982, for example, would have been a teenager at about the time of the First World War and would have had regular contact with people born seventy or eighty years before. One can visualize the overlap as shown in the figure above. Something that happened in 1855 can still be recalled today by an Islander who had long ago talked to an eyewitness to that event.

Before 1850 the oral tradition is far less detailed. The chain of transmission becomes three or four people long, or more, and many of the details and much of the vitality are lost along the way. Memories rely increasingly on formal written accounts. The few stories from before the mid-nineteenth century that are still heard today seem to have been simmered down to a fairly stock format, a distillation of a number of different first-hand and family versions of events, often fixed at some point in the written accounts of Island history, particularly in Banks's thorough three-volume *History of Martha's Vineyard*.[11]

Gaps in the Data   It did not seem possible to learn anything about deaf individuals who lived before the 1830 census or about those who had died young or had moved off-Island and thus simply were no part of the current oral tradition.

Judge Samuel Sewell had mentioned a deaf man on the Island in 1714, and it seemed likely that the hereditary deafness extended back at least that far. But the lack of written records and oral history indicated that nothing further could be known. The pattern of inherited deafness, the degree to which it affected various aspects of Vineyard life, and records for early deaf Islanders all seemed beyond reach.

However, one wintry day in 1980, I interviewed an extremely knowledgeable woman in her middle eighties. She remembered all about the deaf people who had lived up-Island near her, and she had always thought it strange that people should be so interested in them. I was immediately curious to know what other people had been interested in Vineyard deafness. Did she know their names? "Well," she said, "like that professor from Boston," a man who had come to talk with her mother. This had happened long before she was born, but she distinctly remembered her mother mentioning the professor. Her mother had always said how strange it was that someone should come all the way from Boston to hear about the Vineyard deaf. "There was nothing at all unusual about them, you know," her mother would add.

Bell's Research   In the Dukes County Historical Society Library several months after my discussion with this woman, I found a few notes on Island deafness, written by Alexander Graham Bell. These notes, dated in the early 1880s, indicated that Bell, at that time still a professor of elocution at Boston University, had much more extensive notes and manuscripts on Vineyard deafness.

In addition to his work as an inventor, Bell was very active in American deaf education. In 1883, beginning his first major project following the invention of the telephone, Bell decided to investigate whether deafness was inherited (Bruce 1973)—which was a very controversial question at that time—and if it was inherited, how and why. Bell believed that by scrutinizing the records and establishing the genealogy of every family in New England with two or more deaf children, he would find a pattern.

Relying heavily on the unpublished work of the Island genealogist Richard L. Pease of Edgartown, Bell discovered that the Vineyard had the highest concentration of deafness in New England and that many families with deaf members in other areas of New England were in some way related to former Vineyarders (Bell 1913).[12]

Bell and his assistants combed through the available censuses, many Island deeds, probate records, and oral history for further information on genealogies.[13] Over a four-year period he ventured up-Island to Chilmark several times to talk with deaf Islanders and their families, as well as with elderly residents who could recall the relationships between people in generations past.

Bell was never able to explain why hearing parents sometimes had several deaf children, and vice versa. Because of this failure he eventually abandoned the study of Island genetics, although not before he had amassed a considerable amount of information on the subject, and had made an extensive list of all those Islanders known to have been deaf.

Only a small amount of Bell's data on Vineyard deafness ever appeared in published form. In the 1880s and early 1890s several brief articles were printed in *Science* and *American Annals of the Deaf*. Bell gave testimony on deafness on Martha's Vineyard before The Royal Commission on the Status of the Deaf, Blind, Etcetera in England (Gordon 1892), and he relied heavily on his Vineyard work for his controversial book *Memoir upon the Formation of a Deaf Variety of the Human Race* (1883).

I knew that Bell's original, unpublished study existed in a more extensive form because Charles Banks, in his *History of Martha's Vineyard*, published in 1913, thanked Bell for allowing him access to his notes, which Banks described as "enough to fill a dozen volumes of printed matter in the manuscript" (Banks 1966, 1:8). At one time, three copies of his notes seem to have existed (Bell 1913) and may have been put into manuscript form, although no copy of this has been found. The loose notes had apparently vanished.[14] Finally, a reference in one of Bell's private papers led me to the John Hitz Memorial Library, at the Alexander Graham Bell Foundation in Washington, D.C., where the missing set of Bell's notes on Vineyard deafness was found, packed away in storage in a warehouse.[15]

Bell's research on Vineyard deafness was confined to genealogical materials, which proved more useful than I had expected.[16] His notes and charts confirmed a large number of names and facts that I had known only tentatively through oral history. Bell's information, which like my own was largely gathered from the oral tradition, went back to the 1730s, within fifteen years of Judge Sewell's visit to the Island.

Bell's information after 1850 tallied almost exactly with what I had collected from that period, allowing verification of still-current oral traditions. It also provided the names of several dozen other deaf Islanders who lived much earlier than the time the oldest Islander could recall.

The list of deaf Islanders began to form a logical and consistent pattern. Many of the families listed by Bell were direct ancestors of deaf Islanders I had identified. I was then able to go back through all the Island's written records, few of which Bell had used, and gather a substantial amount of data on the daily lives of deaf people from the seventeenth, eighteenth, and nineteenth centuries. I reviewed census data; birth, marriage, and death records; deeds; probate inventories and wills; tax records; school and military lists; church and town records; newspaper accounts; and ships' logs; as well as many private diaries, journals, and letters. During the course of this research I reviewed all pertinent Island records now known to exist.

Islanders were enthusiastic about my interest in the old Vineyard society and the lives of deaf Vineyarders. People viewed the deafness as simply something that had occasionally happened, and not as something to be ashamed of. They did not hesitate to speak freely and proudly of their ancestors. However, I decided to change the names of deaf individuals who lived in the nineteenth and twentieth centuries to ensure privacy for their families. I did this more because of anthropological convention than because of any necessity to do so, and it should not be construed as an attempt to hide identities on account of any pejorative associations. Many of the people I interviewed insisted that I include the names of their ancestors so that they could show the book to grandchildren and great-grandchildren.

Several colleagues suggested that I change the name of the Island or at least the names of the towns. This seemed to me unnecessary, and the suggestion was rejected out of hand by every Islander with whom I discussed it. For one thing, it would be hard to disguise Martha's Vineyard and the Island towns, but more important, a knowledge of Vineyard history provides a time frame and a social context that is invaluable to understanding how deaf individuals were integrated into the society.

The people I worked with on Martha's Vineyard were pleasant, cooperative, and for the most part, thoroughly enjoyable company. Most took an interest in my research, although I was occasionally at the mercy of local wit. For example, I interviewed one Islander in his late eighties, who was said to be particularly knowledgeable about "life in the old days." For nearly an hour he spoke eloquently of the Island of his boyhood days and recalled many deaf men and women he had known by sight, if not through close experience, since he was a resident of Edgartown, where the Vineyard deafness had died out sooner than it had up-Island. I asked this man if he knew about any mentally retarded individuals on the Island, since Bell, in passing, had mentioned several. Well, he said, getting quite serious, he did recall a few, and he proceeded to give me a list of eight names, none of which I had ever heard mentioned as "feebleminded," to use the local term. Only after checking with several other people did I find out that he had given me the names of every Democrat who used to live on Martha's Vineyard.

Perhaps the seriousness with which most of the Islanders view their oral tradition was best summed up by a ninety-six-year-old woman who turned to Gale Huntington one day and said, "You know, we can tell this girl anything! We're the only ones who really remember how it used to be." Then she added, "We'd better get all the facts right. Soon there'll be no one to remember how life used to be on the Island— and wouldn't that be a shame."

2

• • • • • • • • • • • • • •

The History of
Martha's Vineyard

Martha's Vineyard, the largest island off the coast of New England, covers almost a hundred square miles in area. It lies between 70° 27' and 70° 50' west longitude and 41° 18' and 41° 28' north latitude. Roughly triangular in shape, it measures some twenty-three miles east to west at its greatest length, and almost ten miles north to south.[1] Five miles off the southern coast of Cape Cod at its closest point to the mainland, the Vineyard is much larger than the tiny Elizabeth Island chain and much closer to the mainland than the smaller island of Nantucket.[2]

Indian settlement on the Island extends back at least 4,000 years (Ritchie 1969). At the time of contact with European explorers, it was relatively densely populated by bands of Indians who were related to the Wampanoags of southeastern Massachusetts and Rhode Island.[3] Farmers and fishermen, the tribes of Martha's Vineyard and the adjacent areas of Cape Cod were known to the early white settlers as the South Sea Indians (E. Mayhew 1959). Later, when the European settlers came, there was less overt hostility and open confrontation between Indians and whites than was usual in seventeenth- and eighteenth-century New England. The Indians today continue to play an important part in Vineyard life.

The Island was a significant landmark for navigators, frequently mentioned in the accounts of the early European explorers. Giovanni da Verrazzano noted it in 1524. Bartholomew Gosnold landed on the smaller island of Nomans Land in 1602 and is said to have named it

Watertown

Boston

Atlantic Ocean

Massachusetts
Bay Colony

Scituate

Plymouth
Plantation

Plymouth

Sandwich

Cape Cod   Barnstable

Falmouth

Elizabeth
Islands

Nantucket Sound

Martha's
Vineyard

Nantucket

Southeastern Massachusetts in 1650

Martha's Vineyard for one of his daughters. The name was eventually applied to the much larger adjacent island instead.[4] Samuel de Champlain wrote of sighting the Vineyard in 1606, and it was mentioned in the journals (1611–1614) of the Dutch explorers Adriaen Block and Hendrick Christiaensen. Captain John Smith wrote of it in 1614.

• European Settlement

The first European settlement took place in 1644. Early in that year Governor Winthrop of Boston noted in his journal that "some of Watertown began a plantation at Martha's Vineyard beyond Cape Cod, and divers families going thither" (Winthrop 1953, 11:154).[5] This group of families was leaving the Massachusetts Bay Colony to settle on the Island, which was part of a land patent acquired by their Watertown neighbors Thomas Mayhew, Sr., and his son.

Mayhew, an English merchant originally from Dinton in Wiltshire, had come to Massachusetts with his family in 1631. Ten years later, for forty pounds and a beaver hat, Mayhew purchased the rights to an area not yet settled by Europeans, which included Martha's Vineyard, Nantucket, and the Elizabeth Islands, as well as several smaller, nearby islands. Mayhew chose to settle on the Vineyard. He and his colonists were farmers, and the comparatively rich soil of the Vineyard, along with the mild insular climate, promised good crops and an adequate area for sheep grazing. The Elizabeth Islands were too small for this, and Nantucket was too sandy for good farming.

The site of the first town on the Vineyard was the large and protected harbor in the sandy channel running between the extreme eastern end of the Island and the adjacent island of Chappaquiddick (see Map 2). This "Towne upon the Vineyard" (Banks 1966, 2:13) was the only white settlement on the Island for the next twenty-five years. Later, when it became necessary to distinguish this town from others on the Island, it was referred to as Old Town or Great Harbor. In 1671 the town was officially named Edgartown, after Edgar, Duke of Cambridge, then heir apparent to the British throne.

The Island's early history was relatively peaceful. The population increased gradually through immigration. Because it was not easily accessible to the mainland, the Vineyard never attracted more than a handful of families in any year. Most of the early immigrants came

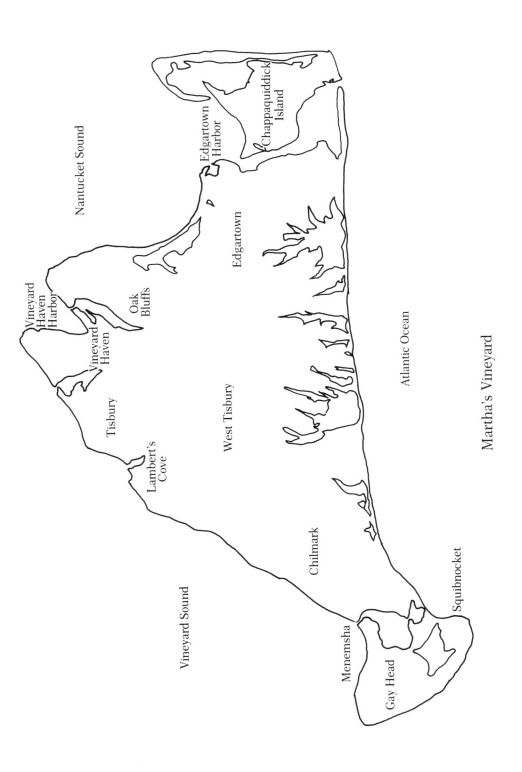

Martha's Vineyard

from the crowded areas around Boston, but in the late 1600s an increasing number came from the lower Cape Cod towns of Sandwich, Barnstable, and Falmouth.

By 1710 immigration had virtually ceased, because much of the land was taken and because large tracts of rich land west of Boston had been opened for settlement. The population of the Island, however, continued to grow rapidly due to a high birth rate and a low death rate.

Tisbury and Chilmark This increasing population put pressure on the available land in Edgartown, and residents began moving up-Island to the area of Middletown, also known by its Indian name, Takemmy. This was a broad, flat area of "fine meadows" in the center of the Island, with rich soil and plenty of water. The name was later changed to Tisbury, after Mayhew's parish in England. By 1680 the settlement had 120 residents (Banks 1966, vol. 2).

Chilmark, also named for an English parish, was the last of the original Island towns to be settled; the actual date of settlement is unclear. Located on the rolling, sandy, western part of Martha's Vineyard, with broad moors and peat bogs, Chilmark was a natural location for sheep raising, which had become a profitable industry in Connecticut and Rhode Island. It was not until the close of the seventeenth century that an "appreciable" population—about forty people—had moved into the area (Banks 1966, 2:5).

In 1691 the Vineyard joined the Commonwealth of Massachusetts, ending years of arguments and strife between the Mahyew family and others who wanted some say in the Island's governing. From then until the middle of the eighteenth century, outside events seemed to have little influence on Vineyard life. But the growing population was placing a strain on the Island's natural resources, especially its farm lands. Although the soil was adequate for the first few generations, overuse and bad crop management caused it to deteriorate rapidly. So this island of farmers, who had no experience of seafaring or fishing, turned to the sea. Within a few generations a number of Vineyarders owned vessels and fished or carried cargo.

The Revolution During the Revolution most Vineyarders strongly backed Washington and his troops, but the Continental Congress was unable to protect the outlying Island. The Vineyard was forced to declare itself a neutral zone, but its ships continued to harass the British navy along the coast. In retaliation British vessels interfered continually with Vineyard trade and traffic and also made several raids for food and supplies, which devastated the Island's economy (Banks 1966, vol. 1).

• The Vineyard as a Maritime Power

After the Revolution the Island's economy was in crisis. The soil was now badly depleted, and sheep raising, still very important, required a great deal of land. Maritime resources became paramount for the first time. Many Vineyard men manned their own whaling ships, and others joined the crews of Nantucket or New Bedford vessels. When de Crèvecoeur visited the Island at the close of the eighteenth century, he wrote, "This island therefore, like Nantucket, is become a great nursery which supplies with pilots and seamen the numerous coasters with which this extended part of America abounds. Go where you will from Nova Scotia to Mississippi, you will find almost everywhere some native of these two islands employed in seafaring occupations" (1957:115).

Within a generation after the Revolution, most facets of Island life were affected by this reorientation to the sea. Devon wrote: "Out of a population of 3,000 on the island, about 5 or 600 cannot be said to have a home upon the land, but go down and not only go down, but live upon the sea in ships and do business, most venturous business, upon the great waters" (1838:11). The ships and sailors of Martha's Vineyard and Nantucket became famous around the world:

> War vessels of European nations, bound on what they thought were voyages of discovery would find some enterprising whaler or sealer from [Martha's Vineyard or Nantucket] . . . calmly riding at anchor in the lea of a coral atoll which they were about to claim for their sovereigns by right of first discovery. And upon questioning these absurd little apple-bowed craft, the crestfallen commanders would learn that this was merely a safe harbor which they had long frequented for repairs, after still further voyages to the remoter Antartic regions (Banks 1966, 1:443).

Island sailors would meet their neighbors in the middle of the Arctic Ocean or on a crowded byway in China. There was a Vineyard Street in Honolulu, and it was said that Vineyarders on some far-flung Polynesian atoll would find young children named after whalers they knew from home (usually for a very good reason).

Edgartown, with the best harbor on the island, was the center of the whaling industry and one of the major ports of New England. Always somewhat less isolated than other areas of the Island, with whaling and the flourishing coaster trade, the town became, by Vineyard standards, positively cosmopolitan. The first issue of the *Vineyard Gazette,* in May 1846, carried a small announcement for families of whalemen who might wish to send a letter to the Pacific Ocean: "For South Seas—Ship Alabama, Capt. Benj. Coggshall, will sail about the 24th of May. Letter bag at this office." Another notice read: "Died— In this town, on the 16th inst., a native of Rarotonga, known by the name of James, late of ship Splendid, aged about 26."

Many men on the Island made their living as fishermen, and others sailed coasting schooners, delivering cargo up and down the east coast. Through Vineyard Sound flowed all of the coastwise traffic both north to the New England states and south to New York, the middle Atlantic, and the southern states. Until the early twentieth century, when the Cape Cod canal made it unnecessary to travel around Cape Cod by way of Nantucket Sound, this body of water was second only to the English Channel in the number of vessels that annually sailed through it.[6]

But the sea took a heavy toll on Islanders. As Huntington (1969) pointed out, many of the headstones in Vineyard cemeteries are only markers, remembrances of men lost at sea. The journals of the Edgartown parsons Kingsbury and Thaxter often recorded three or four deaths when a ship, which may have been away for a year or two, came home. Accidents at sea were the leading cause of death for males in all but the very oldest age groups (Groce 1983).

Only two Island towns did not depend primarily on the sea. West Tisbury, in the center of the Island, maintained its tradition as a farming and sheep-raising community. Many Tisbury men did go to sea, but they retired to the family homestead. Thus some of the Edgartown "whale oil money" also made its way up-Island. Music Street, which runs past the West Tisbury Congregational Church was so named because every house "could boast a piano, all bought with whaling money." Lest this sound too idyllic, it might do to mention that Music Street was also known unofficially as Cowturd Lane (Huntington 1969).

Chilmark, at the western end of the Island, the most remote of the original three towns, depended least on the sea. For almost two hundred years, its economy rested heavily on sheep raising, the most profitable form of Island farming. Miles of "lace fences"—stone walls built to contain sheep—still run off into the underbrush, outlining what were once close-cropped pastures.

Almost everyone in Chilmark lived on a farm that produced food for their families, and many raised crops or dairy cows in addition to sheep. A sizable proportion of the male population added to their farm income by fishing, usually in dories. One man to a boat, they would push off into the pounding surf of South Beach for a day's fishing, returning at night with cod, bluefish, and flounder. The lack of a safe port for larger boats, the local subsistence economy, and the full day's journey to Edgartown over rough and at times dangerous roads made Chilmark isolated, even compared to the other Vineyard towns. Most people in town were able to get by, but few got rich.

• The Twentieth Century

The great days of Vineyard whaling, from the 1820s to the 1860s, were all but gone by the 1890s. After 1859, when petroleum was discovered in Pennsylvania, the Island's economy slowly declined, following the fortunes of the dying whaling industry. At the same time the wool industry was edged out by imports of cheap wool from Australia and New Zealand, which poured into the American textile market. The coasting schooner trade began to flag by the turn of the century, as trains began carrying more and more freight. Fishing filled some of the gap left by whaling, sheep raising, and coasting, but could not completely replace them.

Independent fishermen and lobstermen still sail from Vineyard ports, but their economic significance has long been overshadowed by tourism. In 1835 the first Methodist camp meeting came to the Island; sixty-five people came to worship in the newly introduced Methodist fashion, and nine tents were set up to accommodate them. By 1848 there were fifty tents, and by 1858 three hundred twenty. Word spread quickly of the camp meeting, and the oak grove on the bluffs over-looking Vineyard Sound soon attracted thousands of off-Islanders each summer. By the 1860s the crowds were enormous. In 1878 one summer Sunday crowd was estimated at 20,000 (Banks 1966, vol. 2).

On the outskirts of the camp meeting rose luxurious boarding houses, private summer homes, restaurants, and bazaars for the less religious visitors. Street vendors hawked their wares, a merry-go-round was installed next to the ferry landing, and the boardwalk along the cliffs was always crowded. The settlement that sprang up around the camp meeting grounds was named Cottage City, and in 1888 it became a separate town. In 1909 the name was changed to Oak Bluffs.

Today many people from off-Island come to the Vineyard for vacations, and many retire there to live year-round. Such people have bought and renovated many of the older houses and farms, giving much of the Island a prosperous facade, which hides the fact that the per capita income of native Vineyarders is among the very lowest in Massachusetts. But for all this, many aspects of Island life are still the same as in earlier times.

The old Vineyard families have not disappeared. The descendants of the original settlers still make up a large part, if not the majority, of the year-round population. It was from the elderly members of these families that I collected much of my information.

3

The Origins of Vineyard Deafness

In the latter part of the nineteenth century Martha's Vineyard was well known throughout the country for its whaling and fishing fleets, as well as for its growing reputation as a summer colony. The Island was also occasionally a topic of discussion in scientific circles because of the exceptionally high proportion of people who were born deaf.

• Hereditary Deafness

Although few medical records are available, I have been able to identify the type of deafness that occurred on the Island with some precision.[1] It appeared frequently in certain families and not at all in others. Its common occurrence argues against trauma or illness as a cause. Anyone may become deaf through accident or sickness, but when several of a deaf person's siblings are deaf, and several ancestors are known to have been also, the chances that all became deaf as the result of accident or illness are very slim. Moreover, the diseases known to result in deafness would have had to be present in epidemic proportions in each generation to account for the regular appearance of deafness over the course of three centuries. If that had been the case, some oral history of the disease would probably exist. Far more significant, such a disease or diseases would have been very choosy in their effects, bringing deafness only to individuals whose father and mother both were descendants of long-established Island families.[2] In the three hundred years of settlement, only one deaf child was born to a couple in which one partner's family came from off-Island.[3]

Approximately seventy types of hereditary deafness have been identified (Konigsmark 1969); slightly over half of these are associated
with other abnormalities, such as retinitis pigmentosa, abnormalities
of the skin or external ear, albinism, goiter, nephritis, or cardiac anomalies, forming specific syndromes (Konigsmark 1969; Fraser 1976;
Konigsmark and Gorlin 1976). The remaining types of inherited deafness are nonspecific and have no associated abnormalities (Konigsmark 1972). The affected individuals are normal except for their hearing
loss. The Vineyard deafness seems to have fallen into this category;
all of the affected individuals apparently were normal and in good
health but unable to hear sounds in any frequency range. In old photographs of these people one can see that the external ear looks completely normal. The few medical and death records I located for known
deaf Islanders show no unifying cause of death and do not indicate
any long-term illnesses associated with specific inherited problems
(Groce 1983).

The pattern of inheritance seems to have been recessive in nature.
Eighty-five percent of all children born deaf on the Island were born
to couples in which both parents were hearing. Where deafness appeared in direct ancestral lines, it would often skip two or three, or in
one case six, generations, as is consistent with a recessive trait. It
affected males and females in approximately equal numbers; I have
managed to identify twenty-nine deaf males and thirty-four deaf females, in addition to nine children listed as deaf for whom no records
of sex are available.

• Genetic Origins

The origin of a trait for deafness that will follow a classical recessive
inheritance pattern presumably begins with a single genetic mutation
in an individual. That is, a gene affecting one aspect of the neural or
anatomic development of the hearing mechanism is altered in such a
way that normal development does not occur. The result of such a
mutation is not evident in that individual, as Mendel showed. The
individual carrying the mutant gene, however, may pass it on to some
or all of his or her children. If a descendant of these children then
mates with another descendant of the person in whom the mutation
first occurred, the offspring may receive a gene for deafness from each
parent, be homozygous for that trait, and thus deaf.

It is possible, but statistically very unlikely, that the same mutation could occur in two individuals; the chances that these two people would eventually mate is even more remote. Indeed, because so many types of recessive deafness exist, and because it is assumed that each parent must be heterozygous for the *identical* form of this deafness for it to appear in their children, geneticists tend to regard the appearance of almost any type of recessive deafness as proof that the parents share a common ancestry (Fraser 1976).[4]

The frequency of congenital deafness on the Vineyard points to more than just a mutation for deafness in one individual. There are two questions to be addressed. First, when did the mutant gene for deafness initially occur? And second, how did this genetic trait spread through the Island population? The Island deafness can be traced back through a complex network of marriages and matings to a particular group of early settlers. All of the deaf Vineyarders had some direct ancestral tie to a group of families who settled on Martha's Vineyard between 1642 and 1710. There is strong evidence, however, that the recessive gene for deafness did not occur first in an Islander but in an earlier person whose descendants settled there. It is impossible to know who that person was, or when he or she lived; the mutation may very well have occurred centuries before the settlement of New England. But it is possible to say where, within about ten miles, this person lived and to trace the descendants with a good deal of accuracy.

• Early Vineyard Deafness

On April 5, 1714, Judge Samuel Sewell of Boston, along with some other men, crossed Vineyard Sound to the Island. After the long and tedious trip by boat, the judge engaged a group of fishermen to guide them to Edgartown. Later he noted in his diary, "We were ready to be offended that an Englishman . . . in the company spake not a word to us. But it seems he is deaf and dumb" (Sewell 1972:432). The Englishman mentioned by Sewell was Jonathan Lambert, and he was indeed deaf, as were two of his seven children. His was the first case of deafness recorded on Martha's Vineyard.

Lambert was born in the town of Barnstable on Cape Cod on April 28, 1657, the son of Joshua Lambert, an innkeeper, and his wife, Abigail Linnell. Jonathan moved to the Island in 1694, settling in

Tisbury. His wife's family had already moved there from Barnstable several years earlier, which undoubtedly influenced his decision to settle nearby.

When beginning this research, I anticipated that Lambert, who figures prominently in the subsequent pedigrees of a number of deaf individuals on the Island, would be the one person to whom all of the deafness could be traced. But the original mutation for deafness could not have taken place in Lambert himself for, as already noted, such a trait will appear only in the descendants of the individual in whom the mutation originated. Nor could the mutation for deafness have originated in either of Lambert's parents, for both must have been carriers of the recessive trait in order for it to have appeared in their son. Lambert's father and mother must have had a common ancestor who carried the trait.

Nor does the puzzle end there. Lambert's will, probated in 1738, mentioned "my two Poor children that cannot speake for themselves" (Banks 1966, 2:53), indicating that two of his seven children, who were fifty and thirty-four at the time of Lambert's death, were deaf. For Lambert's children to have been born deaf, his wife (who as far as I know was hearing), must also have carried the same gene for deafness. Hence both Lambert and his wife must have shared at least one common ancestor.

One explanation might be that Jonathan Lambert's parents, in addition to being related to each other, could also have been related to one or both of their daughter-in-law's parents. But I could not find any direct connection between Lambert's father or mother and his wife's father or mother. However, a close affiliation between people born in the same generation in Barnstable, a community of some two hundred people (Trayser 1939), is certainly plausible.

If this lack of evidence of consanguinity between Lambert's family and his wife's were the only unknown factor in the pedigrees of the deaf Vineyarders, I could say with some confidence that a direct ancestor of Lambert and his wife was the index person for Vineyard deafness. But as I investigated the Lambert family pedigree further, the pattern of inheritance became more complicated still. Lambert's sister, who was hearing, married around 1686. Her husband, also from Barnstable, was hearing, as were all their children. One daughter, named Thankful, married her first cousin Ebenezar, her father's brother's son. Of the eleven children born to Thankful and Ebenezar, two sons and a daughter were born deaf. For this to have happened, at least one of Thankful's paternal grandparents and one of her maternal grandparents (the elder Lamberts), must have been carriers for the gene for deafness as shown in the genealogical chart. For this pattern of deafness to have occurred, *a minimum* of four individuals in the first generation shown in the chart below must have been carriers for the gene.

This was not the only puzzle in the ancestry of the Vineyard deaf. Tracing all those affected back to their earliest Island ancestors, I found that only nine of the seventy-two deaf individuals I have identified had either Lambert or his wife in their family trees. But another name, which appeared in sixty-three of the pedigrees, was that of James Skiffe, a hearing man who settled in Sandwich, Massachusetts, with his family in 1633. Skiffe himself never moved to Martha's Vineyard, but a number of his children eventually settled in Tisbury and Chil-

Lambert family genealogy

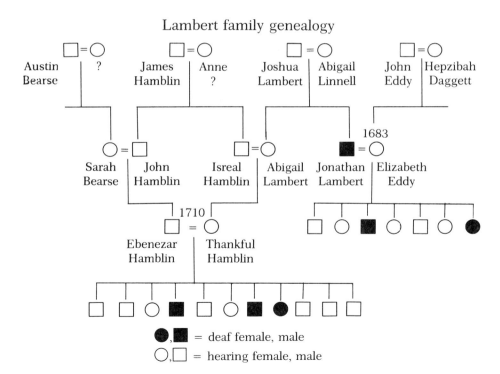

● ,■ = deaf female, male
○ ,□ = hearing female, male

mark. In addition, thirty-two of the deaf Islanders were descendants of a man named Tilton, who had come to the Vineyard about 1673. Most of the deaf Vineyarders had all three of these colonists in their pedigrees, and a dozen other surnames appeared somewhat less frequently in many of the ancestries. I found no direct consanguineal connections among Lambert, Tilton, and Skiffe or their families before they or their descendants moved to the Vineyard.

The likelihood that all these early settlers carried a gene for deafness is strengthened by the fact that marriages between descendants of Lambert, Skiffe, Tilton, and the others also resulted in deaf offspring, even when the parents of a deaf child were connected lineally only once to each of the ancestors.[5]

To make sense of this, I had to find some connection among these early families. I anticipated that the pattern of deafness would be accounted for by marriages between members of these families on Cape Cod during the 1660s and 1670s, and I assumed that a common ancestor would be identified. However, although many of these people almost certainly knew each other before moving to Martha's Vineyard, none of them in that generation were related.

Yet in the end, I found that almost all of these families were, in fact, linked. From 1634 to 1644 all of the families had lived together in the southeastern Massachusetts town of Scituate, the second oldest town in Plymouth Colony. That their descendants had remained near each other as they moved on to the newly opened areas of Cape Cod is not surprising. After all, these families had come to the New World from the same small group of isolated parishes in an area of the English county of Kent known as the Weald. In fact, almost all of them had come over on the same boat.

The pattern of deafness that subsequently appeared indicates that the genetic mutation must have first occurred in someone who lived in the Kentish Weald. In order for the trait to be carried by so many of the early Vineyard settlers, the gene must have been widespread throughout the Kentish population, and so must have existed for a considerable time prior to the seventeenth century.

Once the initial gene for deafness occurred, it was perpetuated by the ingrown nature of rural English villages, particularly in the Weald. It is important, therefore, to take a brief look at the villages of the Weald.

• The Kentish Weald

Extending over parts of east and west Kent (see Map 3), the Weald (old English for "woodland") is usually divided into the high Weald and the low Weald, reflecting local differences in geography and history (Bignell 1975). The sparsely settled high Weald in the west is still heavily wooded and used primarily for grazing cattle. The once-dense forests of the low Weald gradually gave way to small farms as the region was settled in the early Middle Ages (Hasted 1797, vol. 1; Chalkins 1965).

By the seventeenth century, the economy of the low Weald was based on small-scale agriculture and the raising of sheep and cattle (Everitt 1966) along with the manufacture of cloth and iron. Most residents of the low Weald lived on small, individually owned farms. Less than thirty miles in circumference, this small region was divided into over seventy parishes. The countryside was dotted with small hamlets, each one built around a central green or, more commonly, along a well-traveled road (Chalkins 1965). Some villages were trading centers for two or three neighboring parishes. The market towns, which were only slightly larger than the hamlets, usually with less than a thousand people, served the smaller enclaves within a radius of about three to five miles.

Heavily wooded, sparsely settled, with no access to river or sea and having notoriously bad roads, the low Weald was an especially isolated region. An average person could expect to pass his entire life within walking distance of his ancestors' graves. It is certain that some in-breeding—that is, matings between individuals who had at least one common ancestor—existed. Clark, discussing Kentish society, noted that "One important force binding at least respectable villagers to-gether was kinship; almost all young people found their marriage part-ners from the same village or an adjoining one" (1977:121). A number of contemporary writers mentioned how unusually isolated and inbred the population of this area was. Unfortunately, it is almost impossible to document the extent of this inbreeding; in England, births and marriages among the poor and middle classes were not well recorded, and these were the very people who made up most of the emigrants to the New World. Documentation in the Weald existed only for the local gentry, who were much more likely to marry someone from out-side their region than were members of the lower classes. In the Weald,

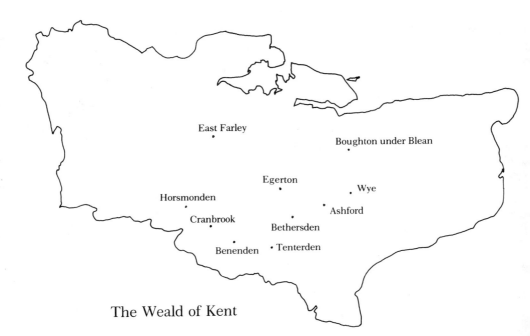

East Farley

Boughton under Blean

Egerton

Wye

Horsmonden

Ashford

Cranbrook

Bethersden

Benenden

Tenterden

The Weald of Kent

however, endogamous marriage was the common pattern even among the gentry to an extent that has attracted the attention of more than one historian.[6]

The Weald as an Isolated Gene Pool   Genetically, the villages, or groups of villages, of the Weald can be considered gene pools. Individuals were not strictly limited to marrying within their own parish or village, but potential marriage partners seldom lived beyond the limits of foot or horse travel. A person's familiarity with the local area, circumscribed by well-known roads and personal networks, has been described as "neighborhood knowledge" (Boyce, Kuchemann, and Harrison 1976a). This was the area from which most marriage partners were chosen. As these authors have succinctly put it, "Marriage distance determines the magnitude of the gene pool" (1976b:264).

In the seventeenth-century village studied by Boyce, Kuchemann, and Harrison, a third of those who married chose partners from outside of the village, but almost all the outsiders lived within a six- to eight-mile radius and probably came from the same village as the partner's mother, grandmother, or some other relative.[7]

According to this pattern, the seventeenth-century English countryside can be seen as a series of semirestricted gene pools. The genetic nature of the population would change gradually as one traveled from north to south or from east to west. The people of each village would be in some way genetically unique yet more similar to people in nearby villages than to those at the other end of the county or in another part of England. Geographically or culturally isolated areas would be more genetically distinct than areas where travel was easy. This situation can be thought of as a genetic continuum rather than as a series of distinct gene pools. But in an isolated regional cluster of hamlets or parishes whose residents intermarried, an altered gene could, over the course of several generations or several centuries, spread widely through the immediate neighborhood. The genetic anomaly would not tend to disappear unless endogamous patterns of marriage and mating changed. Such was the case in the Weald.

• Deafness in the Weald

Although I have been unable to discover any direct references to deafness in the Weald during the seventeenth century, there is some circumstantial evidence concerning deafness during that period. The strongest suggestion involves Sir George Downing, an English politician, for whom London's Downing Street was named. Downing, whose activities for the government included running a series of spy networks, was reputed to have employed a number of deaf people, who reported directly to him. From a passage in Samuel Pepys's diary, it is clear that Downing knew a sign language.[8] During a party in London on November 9, 1666, Pepys and others anxiously awaited news of the fire that was beginning to rage in various parts of the city. Downing was also at the party when a messenger arrived: "There comes in that dumb boy . . . who is mightly acquainted here and with Downing; and he made strange signs of the fire, and how the King was abroad, and many things they understood but I could not, which I wondering at, and discoursing with Downing about it, 'Why,' says he, 'it is only a little use, and you will understand him and make him understand you, with as much ease as may be.' "

Downing, the nephew of John Winthrop, had spent some time in the New World and had attended Harvard College before returning to England. There is no evidence that Downing had contact with anyone from Cape Cod or the Vineyard during these few years, however.[9] Of far more significance here is the fact that Downing had grown up in the small market town of Maidstone in the very heart of the Kentish Weald. It seems likely that as a boy in Maidstone in the 1630s he learned the local sign language. If that is the case, it indicates not only that a sign language was used in Kent, but also that hearing individuals learned it. The later easy acceptance of sign language on the Vineyard may in fact be rooted in its acceptance in such places as Maidstone. It was only a few years later that inhabitants of that very town and the surrounding area left for the New World, to settle eventually on the Vineyard.

A thorough investigation of Kentish census records from the fourteenth century on may tell us even more about the existence of deafness in the Weald. A colleague and I made a fairly thorough inspection of the early records but found no references to deafness; a quick review of late nineteenth- and early twentieth-century data, however, seems to indicate an unusually high incidence of deafness in the population. When my current research is completed, I hope to have a more coherent picture of deafness in the Weald itself.

• Puritanism

I assume here that a trait for deafness had appeared in the Weald by at least the beginning of the seventeenth century. To see how it became important on Martha's Vineyard we must trace the movement of the people of Kent from the Weald to the Island. What induced a group of families from such an isolated region to suddenly pull up stakes and move to an island across the Atlantic?

Their reasons were both religious and economic. The English Puritan movement of the sixteenth and seventeenth centuries was a major force in the Weald; the inhabitants had long been "noted for heterodox opinions" (Furley 1871:377). As early as 1420 a Puritan movement was active in the villages of Benenden, Cranbrook, Smarden, and Staplehurst; and another such movement appears to have arisen in various areas of Kent in the 1590s (Clark 1977). By the seventeenth century the Weald was a prominent center of rural Puritanism.[10] As Chalkins noted, "It was called the receptacle of all schism and rebellion" (1965:228).

Most of the members of this movement were from the lower levels of respectable society—farmers, craftsmen, artisans, and small merchants (Chalkins 1965; Clark 1977). Puritan congregations drew people from a relatively restricted area. Almost all the active separatist congregations lay within a radius of fifteen miles, the most active being in the parish of Egerton (Clark 1977). In the early 1600s these active congregations were increasingly harassed and persecuted.

At the same time the cloth industry, a mainstay of the Wealden economy, was gradually losing ground. From 1614 to 1616, in 1622, and again in 1630 and 1631, the industry underwent major depressions (Chalkins 1965). A good indication of how hard times were becoming throughout the region is given by the percentage of the population who could pay the hearth tax. During the depression years 36 percent of all persons in the Weald were excused from this obligation because of poverty, one of the highest rates in all of Kent (Chalkins 1965). The lack of arable land made it difficult for the unemployed cloth workers to turn to agriculture to make ends meet (Furley 1871; Clark 1977). It is from this area, the center of the cloth-making industry, where economic difficulties intersected with religious unrest, that the future residents of Scituate would come.

By the 1630s a steady stream of settlers was leaving for the New World, firm in the hope of establishing a more perfect church and a better standard of living. Among those who left the Weald in the 1630s were "several companies of Wealden Clothiers, hempdressers and others" (Everitt 1966:60). One congregation, based in the parish of Egerton, with some members from surrounding parishes, left in 1634 with their minister, Reverend John Lothrop.[11] They were on their way to Scituate.

• From the Weald to the Vineyard

In September 1634 John Winthrop, governor of the Massachusetts Bay Colony, who paid close attention to the comings and goings in Boston Harbor, mentioned in his journal: "The Griffin and another ship now arriving with about 200 passengers and one hundred cattle. Mr. Lothrop and Mr. Simmes, two godly ministers coming in the same ship" (Winthrop 1953, 2:134). Among the other passengers on this ship and on the vessel *Hercules,* which arrived shortly thereafter, were thirty members of Lothrop's congregation. The group apparently planned to go directly to Scituate, 32 miles south of Boston. They arrived in Boston Harbor on September 18, and by September 27, almost all of them had arrived in Scituate, where "a considerable settlement had already been made by 'the men of Kent' who received Mr. Lothrop as a former acquaintance" (Deane 1831:168).[12]

Four former members of Lothrop's congregation were among the original founders of Scituate (Groce 1983). Lothrop mentioned in his diary that "upon January 8, 1634/5 Wee had a day of humiliation and then att night joined in covenent togeather, so many of us as had beene in Covenenaunt [sic] before" (Trayser 1939:5).

James Cudworth, a member of Lothrop's London congregation who had arrived in Scituate a year earlier, indicated that Lothrop's group had long been expected there. He wrote to a friend in England: "The Lord has bine very gracious . . . to bringe us oure Pastor whom we so long expected—Mr. Lothrop, who the Lord has brought us in safety" (Pratt 1929:215).

Of the thirty men who are known to have traveled with Lothrop to Scituate (Deane 1831), only two are known to have been single. Eight are known to have been married; they were accompanied to the New

World by their wives and children and nineteen servants—some sixty people. If the remaining twenty men had a similar number of servants and family members, one can estimate Lothrop's group to have numbered about 210.[13] This estimate may be too high; there is no way of knowing. But half of that number would still represent a significant group of people from the same small area of England.

"Men of Kent" continued to arrive in Scituate throughout the fall of 1634 and the early winter of 1635, coming both from Kent itself and from other areas of New England where they had settled temporarily over the previous decade. By February 1635 the town's population had so increased that more land was granted to Mr Lothrop's group (Damon 1884). Settlers from Kent continued to arrive for the next four years, many to join relatives. The family connections are difficult to establish,[14] as records are incomplete, but it is certain that a great number were from neighboring towns in the Weald.[15] A strong case can be made that many of these people shared a common genetic heritage.

By 1636 Scituate was a "compact little settlement" of perhaps twenty-seven households (Pratt 1929), and by 1640 there were fifty or more houses (Trayser 1939). The population remained prominently Kentish in origin (Groce 1983); both in 1635 and in 1640, almost half of the population was from the Weald.[16]

Scituate to Barnstable   Unfortunately the community at Scituate did not remain peaceful for even a decade. In 1638, only four years after Lothrop's arrival, a full-scale dispute arose concerning baptismal practices (Pratt 1929). This problem had been a bone of contention in England (Deane 1831), and the Scituate congregation still considered the difference of enough importance that: "Mr. Lothrop with the greater part of his church, removed to Barnstable in 1639 ostensibly for the benefit of the 'hay grounds' that is, the salt marshes, but probably with a view also to avoid the agitations which began to trouble his church and people" (Deane 1831:59).

Many of the original Kentish contingent went with their pastor to the newly opened township, one of the three original towns on Cape Cod.[17] Plymouth granted permission for the "seating of a congregation" there in 1639, and Lothrop and his followers were settled in Barnstable by October (Deyo 1890).

We do not know the exact number of settlers in early Barnstable, but my research indicates that twenty-five families probably formed the original population (Deyo 1890). All but four of these families had been part of the earlier group at Scituate, so most of the settlers of Barnstable were still the men of Kent.[18]

Barnstable continued to grow, but the Kentish contingent remained the single largest regional group in town.[19] Of the fifty-three men listed in the town records in 1640, twenty were definitely of Kent, and another sixteen may eventually be traced back to Kent. The remainder came from widely scattered regions of England. Five years later the percentage of the town population that was definitely of Kentish origin had risen to about 40 percent.[20] Otis (1888, 1:522) stated that during these early years the town was "predominantly Kentish . . . as nearly all the first settlers of Barnstable came from London or the County of Kent."

Although an increasing number of the town's settlers were from the Massachusetts Bay Colony, the Kentish group was quite isolated from them. Houses in the new settlement were grouped in two separate enclaves. The houses of settlers from the Boston area were clustered around Coggins Pond, while the Kentish group lived some distance away in the neighborhood of Cobb's Hill (Trayser 1939). Whether this settlement pattern was intentional is not known.

The marriage records indicate that this concentrated settlement pattern encouraged continuing intermarriage among children and grandchildren of the original Kentish contingent. Similar backgrounds, customs, family ties, and friendship probably played a part in this, but most important, the group of eligible marriage partners was not large.

The high birth rate and relatively low infant mortality found in this population in Barnstable led to a continuing need for more land. By the next generation, many descendants of people who had originally come from the Kentish Weald had moved into the nearby towns of Sandwich and Falmouth, which in turn became, by seventeenth-century standards, crowded (Groce 1983).[21] Still more land was needed, and another option looked good to many. From the Falmouth headlands one could look southward across Vineyard Sound to the sparsely settled island of Martha's Vineyard, where fertile land was available and cheap. In the 1650s and 1660s some families from the lower Cape Cod region decided to find out more about it.

Settlement on Martha's Vineyard   The initial settlement of Martha's Vineyard in 1644 consisted of some sixty-five people. These first settlers from Watertown had originally come from scattered areas of England, and none are known to have been directly related to each other before they arrived on the Vineyard.[22] They were not carriers of the gene for deafness. Until they began intermarrying with the Kentish families, no deaf individuals were born to them.

Martha's Vineyard was settled gradually, and several dozen families from Sandwich, Barnstable, and Falmouth arrived over the course of the next generation.[23] Although several of these families were from Kent, this portion of the population remained fairly small until 1669. In the summer of that year land in the central portion of the Island was sold to four speculators from the mainland. Two of them, James Allen and James Skiffe, were men of Kent from Sandwich. They may have known about the Island from the several members of Lothrop's original group who had already moved to Edgartown. Allen and Skiffe soon settled on their land, selling the remaining tracts to friends and neighbors from Cape Cod. Eleven settlers, with nine different surnames, came to Tisbury in the early 1670s; six of the families were originally from the Kentish Weald.[24]

In the 1670s and 1680s people from the upper Cape Cod region, along with younger sons of families from both Edgartown and Tisbury, ventured into the Chilmark area (Banks 1966). A significant number had a Kentish heritage, just as had been the case in Tisbury.[25]

The birth rate on Martha's Vineyard was high, particularly in the first two generations of settlement, probably because the first settlers included many young married couples.[26] Also the death rate was significantly lower than it had been in Europe, the largest difference being in the number of children who lived to child-bearing age. The population of the Island reached some 400 by 1700 and leveled off only after 1800 at about 3,100. It stayed about the same until the early years of the twentieth century.[27]

• • • • • • • • • • • • • •

4

The Genetics of
Vineyard Deafness

Immigration to the Island virtually ceased after 1710, and regular contact and intermarriage with those who lived off-Island decreased. From its earliest days, travel to and from Martha's Vineyard was slow, difficult, and irregular. Islanders had little need to travel off-Island because they were economically self-sufficient, except for a few colonial luxuries like sugar, spices, coffee, tea, and rum. The Vineyard needed no food and few manufactured items from the mainland.

Not until the early 1800s was a regular packet service established to the mainland, and only in the 1830s was there more than one boat a day. Even with regular service, travel to and from the Island was haphazard, particularly in winter when the ferries often did not run for long periods of time. In bad winters ice in the harbor was a real problem. Even in an era when people on the mainland did not regularly travel great distances, the degree of isolation on the Vineyard was regularly commented on by natives and visitors alike.

This isolation gave the Island a "distant . . . old-fashioned air." In 1782 Crèvecoeur wrote: "Where ever I went I found a simplicity of diction and manners, rather more primitive and rigid than I expected; and I soon perceived that it proceeded from their secluded situation, which had prevented them from mixing with others" ([1782] 1957:128). But he was quick to add that this did not mean the good citizens of the Vineyard lived in a cultural backwater: "I observed the same calm appearance as among the inhabitants on the continent; here I found without gloom, a decorum and reserve so natural to them, that I thought myself in Philadelphia."

Residents rarely moved off-Island. Jeremiah Pease, writing of his married sister's departure for her new home on Nantucket, spoke of her in the past tense, as if dead: "May 23, [1820] Wind Southwest. This day our sister Velina goes to Nantucket. The parting was truely affecting. She was a fine girl, pleasant disposition and much respected by all her acquaintants. The loss of her agreeable company is very great although married to a fine young man" ([1820] 1974:45). In the nineteenth century it was said that more Island men had been to China than to Boston, only eighty miles away. Until the Civil War, town records continued to record some money matters in pounds, shillings, and pence, and the British system was also used in much local correspondence.

The Island continued to be isolated well into the twentieth century. Today many Islanders venture to the mainland only rarely. Even the regional dialect is markedly different from that on the surrounding mainland; Islanders distinctly pronounce the final and the preconsonantal /r/, although the adjacent areas of Massachusetts and Rhode Island are /r/-less, and they retain the New England short /o/, long gone on most of the nearby mainland (Labov 1972). A number of lexical survivals, now absent from most of the rest of New England, are also still current in the Vineyard vocabulary, such as "spider" for frying pan, "tinker" for a device used to take a hot pan off the stove, "bannock" for a fried cornmeal cake, and "buttery" for pantry (Kurath 1970:23). The plural "housen" for "houses," which according to the *Oxford English Dictionary* was common in England only between 1550 and 1700 (and has not been reported in the New World), was in use up-Island within living memory (Lord 1964:144). The word "tempest" for a very bad storm is still used by many older Islanders.

• The Vineyard as a Genetic Isolate

The isolation of the population was also reflected genetically. All of the forty-eight major families on the Island had arrived by 1710. James Freeman, in a report published in 1807, noted: "As Martha's Vineyard receives not many accessions of inhabitants from abroad, the names of its families which have sprung from the original settlers of the island are few in number. Thirty-two names comprehend three-quarters of the population" (1971:26), and he gave a chart showing the number of households by surname on the Island at that time: Luce, 41; Norton,

33; Mayhew, 24; Smith, 23; Allen, 19; Pease, 19; Tilton, 19; Butler, 16; Doggett, 14; Dunham, 14; Athearn, 13; Fish, 13; Coffin, 11; Cleaveland, 10; Cottle, 10; Hillman, 10; Look, 10; Vincent, 10; Manter, 9; Merry, 8; Chase, 7; Davis, 7; Merchant, 7; Marchant, 6; Crosby, 5; Gray, 5; Stewart, 5; West, 5; Worth, 5; Adams, 4; Hancock, 4; Wicks, 4. As Crèvecoeur noted, "It is impossible for any traveller to dwell here one month without knowing the heads of the principal families" (p. 123).

Subdivisions within the Population Because of its size, the Vineyard cannot be considered a single gene pool. In the seventeenth and eighteenth centuries family members tended to settle near one another. Many neighborhoods came to be identified with one or two family surnames, and the residents could often trace their ancestry back to a pair of seventeenth-century siblings or first cousins. These neighborhood subisolates were predominantly composed of a handful of families, as is clearly seen in the distribution of the fourteen largest families by town according to the 1850 census. Table 1 gives the number of persons with those family surnames in each Island town.

Table 1. Number of persons in the fourteen largest Island families, 1850.

Name	Town			
	Edgartown	Tisbury	Chilmark	Total
Luce	50	235	15	300
Norton	152	91	15	258
Smith	133	105	13	251
Mayhew	41	41	91	173
Pease	128	17	5	150
Vincent	86	19	10	115
Fisher	106	0	0	106
Tilton	0	12	75	87
West	0	55	25	80
Daggett	12	67	0	79
Coffin	75	0	0	75
Allen	0	25	22	47
Hillman	0	19	24	44
Manter	0	26	9	35

Distance was a significant factor in deciding whom one met and married, as is reflected in oral history and in local records. Before the automobile, Edgartown was a full day's journey from the up-Island towns over rough and sometimes treacherous roads. For up-Islanders, going down-Island was a major event: "You see, when I was young . . . people didn't travel around much. I used to go down town, down to Vineyard Haven once a year, that's all I'd ever go as a kid. I'd go down on my birthday and get a pair of shoes for school. That's the only time I'd go downtown. I'd never go for anything else."

Down-Island at least had the attraction of shops, the ferry, and medical and legal services. For down-Islanders, up-Island was only farm land. "When I was a girl growing up, we didn't travel in cars the way they do today. Up-Island was practically like going to Europe, as far as I was concerned. It was a great treat to go up-Island, to go up to the Cliffs or any place like that. So I had very little contact with up-Islanders."

Travel between adjacent towns, such as Chilmark and West Tisbury, was also infrequent. As one of my informants carefully explained:

> You must remember, when I was little, the towns were further apart than they are now. In my days I remember when, even after I was married, my mother and I would go to West Tisbury to do our marketing, because we didn't have any decent store in Chilmark. We'd have to take the whole day. Oh yes. A horse and wagon, you know. Take a lunch with us and take some grain for the horses—a whole day. Now you make two or three trips a day, you don't think anything about it.

Another informant, now in her nineties, when asked about a family in Chilmark, said: "I don't know much about them. They were in Chilmark, and I never bothered much. See, I was born in West Tisbury." Her house is less than a mile from the Chilmark line.

One man who is now in his late sixties mentioned that even in more recent times adults have been intensely aware of the different sections of Chilmark and of who belonged where. This man decided to marry a woman from another part of Chilmark:

> See, I was incarcerated around [Menemsha] creek for the most part. I didn't ever venture very far from the creek. I come to school, but everyone pretty much stayed in their own bailiwick unless

there was some kind of social function. You know, the North Roaders stayed on the North Road, and the South Roaders stayed on the South Road. There was a lot of feelings, bad feelings, between these parts of town, too . . .

It was just general principle. Well, I know when—'course, I was a creeker, and my wife, she come from the South Road, and God, her father was mad! "Marrying one of them damn creekers," he said. "I never knew a creeker that amounted to anything!" Really mad about it. I was a damn creeker as far as he was concerned, didn't like me at all. Genuine, he wasn't being funny, oh no.

People were most likely to marry someone from their own town, and those who married outside of town were more likely to marry an individual from the adjoining town than from the other end of the Island. The census of 1850 gave information on the number of people who lived in the towns where they were born, as shown in Table 2.

Inbreeding The marriage patterns on the Vineyard were not different from the patterns in rural communities throughout New England. According to Yankee kinship rules, marriages between half siblings or between uncle and niece or aunt and nephew were considered incestuous and were all but unknown. First cousins were known as "own cousins," and although they were considered closely related, there were no sanctions against marriages between them; it was fairly common. Second and third cousins and those still more distantly related commonly married.

Because marriage between cousins was permitted, and because there was very little new blood to choose from on a relatively isolated island,

Table 2. Number of persons living in Island town where born, 1850.

Presently living in	Born in			Total	% native in town
	Edgartown	Tisbury	Chilmark		
Edgartown	1,413	86	10	1,509	93.6
Tisbury	86	1,343	96	1,525	88.8
Chilmark	45	115	486	646	73.6

as generations passed, lines of descent on the Vineyard became entangled. According to the pedigrees I have calculated for this study, by the late 1700s, of those who married, over 96 percent married someone to whom they were already related. As time went on, when cousins married, they often were already double cousins—for example, second cousins through the mother's family and fifth cousins through the father's. By the middle of the nineteenth century, almost 85 percent of the second cousins who married on the Island were also related as third, fourth, or fifth cousins through other lines of descent. Some had as many as eight double-cousin ancestors in twelve generations.

Because of these marriage patterns, within three generations nearly every Island family whose ancestors were not from Kent was linked to a Kentish family by at least one marriage, and often a dozen or more.

Some data can be winnowed from the distribution of Kentish surnames on the Island. In Tisbury half of the first generation born on the Island had one or both parents of Kentish origin; this figure rose to three-quarters by the second generation, as sons and daughters of the non-Kentish group chose Kentish marriage partners. The percentages in Chilmark were even higher. Originally somewhat less than half of the community had a Kentish background, but by the next generation, about 85 percent had one or more ancestors who were "of Kent." In Edgartown only 14 percent of the population was from Kent in the first two decades—a small but continually growing minority.

By the fourth generation almost 90 percent of Tisbury's population and more than 90 percent of the Chilmark population had at least one ancestor from Kent. On the western part of the Island, by the fifth generation, the percentage of those who did not have at least one ancestor with a Kentish surname was negligible.

As inbreeding continued from generation to generation, the frequency of the gene for deafness in the population would be expected to increase. That gene, I have suggested, was widely distributed in the Vineyard population with Kentish ancestry. So the chances of deaf children being born rose with every generation, as the probability of having more than one Kentish ancestor rose.[1] And in fact the number of deaf individuals born on the Island did rise gradually from the late seventeenth century on, peaking in the 1840s at forty-five. At that time almost all of the Island residents had two or more Kentish ancestors.

• The Distribution of Vineyard Deafness

There was a significant amount of deafness in all towns on the Island with the exception of Gay Head, whose population was mostly Indian.[2] But the proportions were not uniform throughout the Vineyard. Edgartown had the smallest number of deaf individuals, in part because a smaller percentage of the residents had Kentish ancestry and in part because the port town always had more contact with the outside world than did the up-Island towns. Especially as the whaling industry grew, new people continually entered the Edgartown population. Because both parents must be carriers of a recessive trait for it to appear in their offspring, it is not surprising that the number of deaf people born in Edgartown decreased from the early nineteenth century onward.

But deafness was not unknown in Edgartown. Sarah Harlock, seamstress, born in 1723, was the first known deaf individual in the town. Thereafter the rate of deafness gradually increased, reaching four times the national average by the late eighteenth century. Six individuals who had been born deaf were alive in the town in 1800, when the population was 1,375. Their numbers began to decline by 1830, and the last one died in 1880. (This date falls at the very outer edge of current oral history, so most of the anecdotes in the following chapters concern deaf people up-Island rather than in Edgartown. However, it should be noted that the social adaptation to deafness found up-Island seems to have been present in Edgartown as well from the seventeenth to the early nineteenth century.)

Tisbury and Chilmark were predominantly Kentish towns from the outset, and from the first generation on, continuing inbreeding led to a rapid growth in the number of deaf individuals. While the average number of deaf people in the Island population as a whole was 1:155, in Tisbury it was 1:49. In 1704 the first known deaf individual, Beulah Lambert, was born in Tisbury; the last one died in 1937. In Chilmark, the most isolated of all Island towns, by the middle of the nineteenth century the number of deaf individuals was 1:25. In one small neighborhood of Chilmark with about sixty people, the rate of deafness was 1:4. In all, in a town whose average population was only 350 from the eighteenth to the twentieth century, 39 individuals are known to have been born deaf.

The deafness that appeared on the Vineyard, then, can be explained genetically in terms of a mutant gene for deafness and subsequent inbreeding by the carriers of that gene, first in the Weald and then on the Vineyard. This group of carriers for deafness was unusually large. In effect the group was a migrating neighborhood that went through three major relocations—from Kent to Scituate, from Scituate to Barnstable and adjoining Cape Cod towns, and from Cape Cod to Martha's Vineyard.

Nor was this the end. In the late eighteenth century, in the economic slump after the Revolution, several dozen Vineyard families left to seek their fortunes as farmers in the Sandy River Valley of Maine, near Farmington; they settled the towns of New Sharon and New Vineyard (Poole 1976). These families stayed in close contact and continued to intermarry. Individuals in this group must have been carriers for deafness, for within three years of their arrival a deaf child was born, the first of several dozen deaf individuals (Groce 1983).

Only in the 1840s, as the new American West began to draw people away from New England in smaller family units, did the descendants of Kentish settlers begin to drift away from the formerly cohesive gene pool whose ancestry can be traced to several small, adjacent English parishes.

• Theories of the Causes of Vineyard Deafness

If there is a clear correlation between marriage patterns on the Island and the appearance of deafness, one might wonder if any attempt was made to alter those patterns to avoid having deaf children. Apparently this was not an issue. At least according to current oral tradition, the possible appearance of deaf children was not considered to be a significant enough problem to prevent a hearing person from marrying a deaf person or someone who was closely related to a deaf person. Nor did it prevent deaf Vineyarders from regularly marrying either hearing or deaf fellow Islanders.

To raise the question presupposes that the Islanders saw a pattern in the occurrence of deafness and believed that it was inherited. In fact, there was no agreement in either lay or scientific circles as to the cause or causes of deafness during the two and a half centuries that deaf children continued to be born on the Island. Heredity, environment, maternal fright, and contagious disease were all advanced by scientists as "the" explanation. The Islanders had no clear idea why deafness occurred (see Appendix B).

Some people claimed, correctly as we now know, that deafness "ran in families," but most Islanders saw, and still see, no pattern to the appearance of deafness. Although most members of the old Island families with whom I talked were acutely aware of their genealogical connections to the original settlers, many were unclear about their exact relationship to more recent relatives who were not in the same direct line of descent. Kinship ties were strongest among lineal descendants, and people were generally acquainted with their first cousins. Although most people were aware of who their second and third cousins were, little attention was paid to these and more distant relatives, who were grouped together under the general category of "cousins." In most of the large families these more remote ties of kinship were only vaguely known or acknowledged.

Because of this, a married couple who had one or more common ancestors often was not aware that inbreeding was occurring (this is known to geneticists as unconscious or hidden inbreeding).[3] People whom I spoke with often insisted they were not related to individuals with the same surname. Up-Island and down-Island several members of the Tilton clan, for example, argued that they were not related at all, although both sections could clearly be traced to the same seventeenth- and eighteenth-century ancestors.

Because of the complexity of family lines and the fact that deafness was not considered particularly unusual, in many cases even a direct descendant of a deaf individual was unaware of the deafness, although he or she usually knew what farm land the deaf person had owned, how many children he had had, when he had lived, and where and how he had died. In at least eight separate families, I was the first person to mention that a great-grandparent was deaf, even though the descendants knew their ancestors' names and a number of stories about them.

For these reasons Islanders saw little pattern to the inherited deafness. At one time everyone in a community would have known that a certain person and his father and his father's father's brother were all deaf, but after the death of the deaf person and his contemporaries, the facts were gradually forgotten. Eventually only the son's deafness may have been remembered. Such situations came up regularly when

I discussed deafness with present-day Islanders. The links showing a clear pattern of hereditary deafness had dissolved, and each individual's deafness was seen as an isolated and unexplained case.

For a long time it was popularly believed that marriage between two closely related people would have deleterious consequences for the offspring. When interest in consanguinity as a cause of deafness began to grow during the 1850s and 1860s, many scholars argued that this folk belief should be taken at face value. In an article calling for responsible medical observation of the children of consanguineous marriages, an anonymous author wrote, in the prestigious *Boston Medical and Surgical Journal:*

> Perhaps statistical evidence to show the safety and propriety of marriages between persons nearly related, might be accumulated; but, as we think, with difficulty. There surely must be some good reason and an adequate foundation for the universally entertained belief that these connections are more or less uniformly unfortunate, either physically, mentally, or morally. There is always a large admixture of truth in what "all the world" believes—to use a common phrase. (1859:523–524)

In 1855 the Reverend Charles Brooks presented a paper before the American Association for the Advancement of Science suggesting a systematic approach to the problem, and he noted that the large deaf community on Martha's Vineyard would be a perfect group on which to test theories of inherited deafness. In 1858 the American Medical Association published a systematic attempt to pull together all the scattered references to consanguineous marriages, with particular emphasis on the occurrence of deafness (Bemiss 1858). Again, Martha's Vineyard was cited in several of these works.

There followed many more papers, increasingly sophisticated in design, as scientists studied congenital and adventitious deafness, marriage between deaf individuals, marriages between hearing and deaf, and marriages of hearing people that resulted in deaf offspring. Other factors examined were birth order, disease, prematurity, problems of medical identification, age of onset of deafness, and whether offspring from consanguineous marriages had a higher probability of being deaf. Many made mention of the deafness on Martha's Vineyard to shore up their various points of view, although no research had actually been done on the Island.[4]

Many argued that questions of heredity had nothing to do with the understanding of deafness. As Fraser noted, the mid to late nineteenth century saw "great philosophical polemics between consanguinists and anticonsanguinists" (1964:120). Anticonsanguinists included the religious, the anti-Darwinists, and a number of scientists who sincerely believed that inherited traits were not a sufficient explanation for deafness. Hawkins, a firm supporter of consanguineous explanations, complained:

> One of the essentially predisposing sources of innate deafness is now generally believed to be the intermarriage of close or blood relationships . . . Yet the open avowal of this doctrine (true as it undoubtedly is) is looked upon as ultra-Malthusian and almost heterodox. Appeal is made to the Scriptures, and the case of Zelophehad's daughters who "were married unto their father's brother's sons," instanced to us as a precedent which God himself had sanctioned and established, in the Pentateuch, under the Mosaic Laws. (Hawkins 1863:iv)

Jenkins, though believing that inherited traits could exist in animals, said: "Man cannot be governed in his selection as animals are controlled, and all analogies from the lower animals to prove the possibility of a deaf mute race are not pertinent when applied to man, for in him the tendency is to fixity and to increased homogeneity" (1891:100). The Irish Census of 1881, the most extensive study of deafness to that date, concluded, "It appears evident that the question of deafness and dumbness in parents has no influence in propagating the defect" (Fay 1898:3).

It was at this point that Alexander Graham Bell decided to investigate hereditary deafness. He reasoned that if deafness was in fact hereditary, a full review of pedigrees would show it. He did not know specifically what he was looking for as he began the largest study on the causes of congenital deafness yet undertaken. As he wrote, "My plan is this, I trace the ancestry up in every branch. I do not know what it is that we are looking for except that it is probably something abnormal. Therefore we search for any peculiarities or abnormalities among ancestors, or the brothers or sisters of ancestors" (1892:12).

Bell and his assistants for four years combed through census and genealogical records, concentrating on New England, where the records were relatively good. Because an unusually large number of deaf people seemed to be concentrated on Martha's Vineyard, particularly in Tisbury and Chilmark, Bell turned his attention to the Island, where he collected reams of notes and piles of genealogies. But he could not make sense out of the patterns of inheritance.

For Bell, as for his predecessors, the confusion was caused by a lack of knowledge of Mendelian genetics. Bell was never able to account for the fact that deaf parents did not always have deaf children and that hearing parents sometimes had children who were born deaf. There seemed to be no logical pattern as to when or why deafness would appear.

Victorian science held that traits were inherited in a direct line from parent to child to grandchild. If a parent, a grandparent, or a more distant direct ancestor was not deaf, there was no reason to suppose that a deaf child had inherited the problem. Other deaf relatives—aunts, uncles, nieces, nephews, cousins close or distant—did not count. The most that could be said was that deafness somehow "ran in families." (See, for example, Orpen 1836; H. Peet 1854; Sedgwick 1861; A. Mitchell 1863; *American Annals of the Deaf* 1890; Gillett 1891; Fay 1898.)

Even Darwin was unable to offer an explanation. "It is a singular fact that, although several deaf-mutes often occur in the same family, and though their cousins and other relations are often in the same condition, yet their parents are rarely deaf-mutes," he wrote in 1868. Darwin concluded, "It is safer in the present state of our knowledge to look at the whole case as simply unintelligible" (1920:454). Not until Gregor Mendel's concept of recessive heredity became known in 1900 did scientists have the key to understanding familial patterns of inheritance.

Although he did not understand how the Vineyard deafness was inherited, Bell seems to have been confident that the problem was tied to heredity, and he argued that marriages between deaf individuals should be discouraged because of the likelihood of deaf offspring. If deafness occurred at such a high rate in a population such as that on Martha's Vineyard, he warned, grouping deaf children together in residential schools would only compound the problem by encouraging even more marriage between deaf partners, eventually leading to a whole race, or "variety" of congenitally deaf people. Bell was not the first scholar to suggest that deaf people refrain from intermarriage (Morris 1861; Turner 1868; Cranfield and Federn 1970), but his statements on this subject brought the issue to public attention and sparked a long and bitter controversy in the deaf community.

The information that Bell gathered on deafness on Martha's Vineyard formed the core of his well-known monograph *Memoir upon the Formation of a Deaf Variety of the Human Race*. Subsequent work by eugenicists, well into the twentieth century, relied heavily on Bell's data to persuade many deaf individuals in the United States not to marry. A number were sterilized, often against their knowledge or will. Yet few of these scholars questioned the data on which Bell based his conclusions. Bell's notes, unavailable until now, clearly show that without a knowledge of the Mendelian concept of recessively inherited traits, many of his conclusions about the appearance of familial deafness are simply incorrect. A meticulous researcher, Bell was not unaware that there was a piece missing from the puzzle. On one scrap of paper I found among his notes, he had jotted down a question to himself. In families in which deafness seemed to run, why was only one child in every four born deaf? As any student of high school biology will recall, the probability of appearance of a recessive Mendelian trait is one in four (25 percent) for each offspring.[5]

• The End of Island Deafness

In fact, the establishment of residential schools, which Bell so feared, was the first step in ending the pattern of recessive deafness in isolated communities such as Martha's Vineyard. Deaf Vineyard children began to be sent away for schooling at the newly founded American Asylum in Connecticut in the 1820s and 1830s, and by the 1860s many of them were staying at the schools until their mid to late teens. A number of them married classmates from elsewhere, whose deafness or hearing problems had a wide variety of causes. Some had been deafened by childhood disease, accident, or unknown causes. Several had recessive forms of deafness, but none shared the same recessive gene as their Vineyard spouses. Hence the offspring of these marriages did not inherit the Vineyard form of deafness. In fact, the probability of these deaf Islanders bearing deaf offspring would have been much higher if they had remained at home and married hearing people, because a high percentage of the hearing Islanders were undoubtedly also carriers of this particular gene for deafness.

Just as important, by the latter part of the nineteenth century, hearing Islanders were beginning to regularly marry off-Islanders. With the decline of whaling, the coastal schooner trade, and sheep raising, many young people left the Vineyard to find work after they finished school. While a number eventually returned home to settle down, many brought their off-Island spouses back with them. In addition, two new groups of people were arriving on the Island: summer people and Portuguese immigrants. Both groups had an impact on the Island's genetic character.

Improved transportation and crowded city life encouraged many well-to-do Victorian families, with their children and servants, to spend summers on Martha's Vineyard, first in Oak Bluffs and Edgartown and eventually in the up-Island towns as well. Some of these visitors stayed on, marrying local people and settling down to raise families.

The Portuguese Azores were a major port of call for New England whaling vessels and a place to hire additional crew members. When the ships returned to New England, some Azoreans decided to stay and to send home for their families. Excellent fishermen, many were attracted to the Vineyard. A large Portuguese group had settled on the Vineyard by the turn of the century, and more would follow. There was some friction between these new immigrants and the Yankees, but the Portuguese slowly began to marry into the older Island families. Neither the summer people nor the Portuguese were carriers of the Island's recessive gene for deafness, and none of these Island/off-Island marriages produced deaf offspring.

As a result of these changes in marriage patterns among both the hearing and the deaf, the number of children who were born deaf declined rapidly. In the 1840s fourteen deaf individuals were born in Chilmark, in a population of about 350. In the 1870s only one deaf child was born in the town. In 1900 there were fifteen deaf people alive on the Island, but by 1925 only four remained, and by 1945 only one. She was to be the last. Because of the number of marriages with off-Islanders over the last several generations, it is unlikely that recessively inherited Island deafness will reappear, although it remains theoretically possible in descendants of the old Island families.

• • • • • • • • • • • • • •

5

The Island Adaptation to Deafness

How does a community with a pattern of hereditary deafness adjust to that disorder? In modern Western societies "handicapped" individuals have been expected to adapt to the ways of the nonhandicapped. But the perception of a handicap, and of its associated physical and social limitations, may be tempered by the community in which it is found. The treatment of the deaf people of Martha's Vineyard is an interesting example of one community's response.

Unlike individuals similarly handicapped on the mainland, deaf Vineyarders were included in all of the community's work and play situations. They were free to marry either hearing or deaf persons. According to tax records, they generally earned an average or above average income (indeed several were wealthy), and they were active in church affairs. Enough can be gleaned from the records, furthermore, to indicate that this situation existed not only in the late nineteenth century but for more than three centuries. This implies that the social attitude was fully accepting of deaf individuals and that it was firmly in place from the time that the first deaf man settled in Tisbury in the 1690s.

• Attitudes toward Deafness

As I have discussed, Vineyarders had no clear understanding why deafness appeared in their families or how it was passed from one generation to the next. Deafness was seen as something that just "sometimes happened"; anyone could have a deaf child. The Vine-yarders' social response to this was a simple acceptance of the inability to hear. This is clearly shown in the responses of my informants to questions about how hearing members of the community treated deaf members. The following replies are representative:

> You'd never hardly know they were deaf and dumb. People up there got so used to them that they didn't take hardly any notice of them.

> It was taken pretty much for granted. It was as if somebody had brown eyes and somebody else had blue. Well, not quite so much— but as if, ah, somebody was lame and somebody had trouble with his wrist.

> They were just like anybody else. I wouldn't be overly kind be-cause they, they'd be sensitive to that. I'd just treat them the way I treated anybody.

The community's attitude can be judged also from the fact that until I asked a direct question on the subject, most of my informants had never even considered anything unusual about the manner in which their deaf townsmen were integrated into the society. They were truly puzzled by an outsider's interest in the subject. Almost all informants believed that every small town in New England probably had a similar number of deaf people and adapted to them in much the same way. Many were genuinely surprised when I told them that the incidence of deafness on the Island was unusually high.

Those few who had wondered about the rate of deafness or the attitude toward Islanders who were deaf had either stumbled across one of the nineteenth-century articles on Vineyard deafness or had spent some time off-Island: "I used to wonder why there was so much deafness, because when I went away to school in Boston, there wasn't anybody around who was deaf. I never saw anybody who was deaf, and I wondered why there wasn't." Another man recalled:

> The only time that I ever thought about it was when I read an article in the Boston paper. I thought it was so funny that they should write about it in the paper . . . It struck me funny that they should have an article, because to me, you know, it was

something very ordinary and I used to think, wasn't it funny that a Boston paper would be interested in it.[1]

I found no disagreement on this subject. Although people's recollections of the "good old days" usually gloss over or ignore the rougher, less appealing aspects of community life, that does not seem to have been the case here. The oral histories I collected hardly lead one to conclude that everyone lived in harmony and was always thoughtful and kind to neighbors and relatives. I heard numerous accounts of feuds, dissension, and strife. Even an occasional murder slipped in. Stories about those who were mentally retarded or mentally ill make it clear that the Vineyard attitude toward these groups a century ago differed little from what is found today in our own society.

Vineyarders did not try to give me an idealized version of how the deaf people were treated; the inability to hear simply did not affect a person's status in the community.

The feelings of the deaf Islanders about being unable to hear are less easily known, since none of them are still alive. Those who remember the deaf Islanders do not recall them saying much about the subject. One woman remembered that her "old maid aunt" regretted being unable to hear. "She rebelled very much because of her inability to hear. Every once in a while she would, she'd say [in signs] 'I hear no, shake-fist-at-God.'" Another woman recalled that her deaf mother would get "terribly frustrated" at times. But this, the woman believed, was because her mother was the last deaf person up-Island, and by that time there were few people left who could communicate with her in sign language.

Most people remembered the deaf as being far more positive about their inability to hear. "I know that I asked him once, I never forgot it, because, well, because it was typical of him. I said, 'Have you ever felt you missed anything important in life because you couldn't speak and hear?' And he said, 'No, I have never had to listen to anything unpleasant.'"

A reporter doing a story for the *Boston Sunday Herald* in 1895 found the deaf Vineyarders unconcerned about their condition:

The kindly and well-informed people whom I saw, strange to say, seem to be proud of the affliction—to regard it as a kind of plume in the hat of the stock. Elsewhere the afflicted are screened as much as possible from public notoriety. But these people gave me a great lot of photographs, extending back four generations. These pictures of people who have never spoken a word from the day of their birth, create the impression of the invasion by deafness of what might otherwise have been a wonderfully perfect type.

Most Vineyarders remembered that those who were deaf regarded their inability to hear as a nuisance rather than an overwhelming problem, an attitude not uncommon among many deaf people (Higgins 1980). Most, when pressed on the point, believed that local people, hearing or deaf, preferred to have hearing children, but the birth of a deaf child was regarded as a minor problem rather than a major misfortune. This apparent lack of grave concern reflected the extent to which Vineyard society had long ago adapted to its indigenous genetic alteration.

• Sign Language on the Island

The entire community up-Island (and, presumably, earlier in the nineteenth century, down-Island as well), was bilingual in English and sign language. As the reporter from the *Boston Sunday Herald* found:

> You make a neighborly call—they don't have such things as afternoon teas. The spoken language and the sign language will be so mingled in the conversation that you pass from one to the other, or use both at once, almost unconsciously. Half the family speak, very probably, half do not, but the mutes are not uncomfortable in their deprivation, the community has adjusted itself to the situation so perfectly. (1895:2)

Learning the Language   The Islanders learned sign language in childhood. When I asked informants how either hearing or deaf children learned to sign, there was general consensus that the growing child learned the language as naturally as he would learn English. Children growing up in households with deaf members "just picked up the language," many people told me. As the daughter of one deaf woman said, "I had never given much thought to that. It came naturally." One elderly man recalled that his hearing cousin, daughter of a deaf father and hearing mother, acquired the use of signs even earlier than speech. "She could talk deaf and dumb with her fingers earlier than she could speak. I've often heard that it started off with her when she was young . . . I know they used to say that she had talked with [her father] earlier than she could talk with her hearing mother."

Research has shown that deaf children exposed to sign language in infancy will begin to sign at least as early as hearing children begin to speak. Some research indicates that the ability to sign may in fact precede the ability to speak by several months.[2] The rate at which deaf children acquire a vocabulary, if they are signers, is virtually identical to the rate of hearing children, and by the age of five or so, both have acquired vocabularies of over 1,000 words. In contrast, a deaf child who is given oral instruction only and is not exposed to sign language often has a functional vocabulary of only several dozen words by the age of five. The acquisition of sign language and English by hearing children of deaf parents has been studied, and it has been found that both languages are easily acquired simultaneously (Prinz and Prinz 1979, 1981).

On the Vineyard, hearing children with no deaf immediate family members learned sign language (which they called "deaf and dumb") by accompanying their parents on daily chores to the neighbors or the store, where they saw signs used regularly. They needed to learn the language to communicate with deaf adults as well as deaf playmates.

In hearing families, as well as those with deaf members, parents introduced their children to sign language. Fluency in the language was reinforced and polished by continual use. One very elderly woman explained, "When I was a little girl, I knew many of the signs and the manual alphabet, of course, but I didn't know how to say 'Merry Christmas,' and I wanted to tell Mr. M. 'Merry Christmas.' So I asked Mrs. M., his wife. She could hear, and she showed me how. And so I wished Mr. M. 'Merry Christmas'—and he was just so delighted." This woman then described how she taught her own son, now in his late seventies, how to speak sign language:

> When my son was perhaps three years old, I taught him to say in sign language "the little cat" and "dog" and "baby." This man, who was deaf, he used to like to go down to our little general store and see people come and go. One day when I went down

there, I took my son there and I said to him, "Go over and say 'how-do-you-do' to Mr. T.," the deaf man. So he went right over, and then I told him to tell Mr. T. so-and-so, a cat, a dog, and whatever. And wasn't Mr. T. tickled! Oh, he was so pleased to know a little bit of a boy like that was telling him all those things, and so he just taught my son a few more words. That's how he learned—that's how we all learned.

None of my informants remembered any formal teaching of sign language. "It was, I'll tell you, I guess it was just a sort of instinct . . . you couldn't help learning it. You would be exposed to it all the time, really." For those who lived up-Island, a knowledge of the language was a necessity. "You had to learn sign language. Everybody knew it . . . they'd have to know it, in order to get along up here." A lady from Edgartown, who regularly visited her aunt, an up-Island native, recalled:

My aunt could talk it just like a deaf and dumb person. Almost everyone spoke it [up-Island], because there were so many deaf and dumb people . . . I seem to have took it for granted that everyone knew how to speak deaf and dumb. It was not unusual at all to see somebody talking deaf and dumb, just somebody else, so it didn't create too much attention. Most of the Vineyarders of that generation knew how to talk it.

In 1931 a column in the *Vineyard Gazette* gave brief biographies of some of the older Islanders. One of those featured was deaf, and the writer noted:

There were a considerable number of deaf and dumb people in Chilmark during Mr. North's boyhood, and this fact no doubt made his life much less lonely than would have been the case had he been born alone with his affliction. He had both brothers and sisters who were deaf like himself, and also those who could speak and hear perfectly. There were numerous others, children and adults, and because of their numbers there were very few people in the town who could not converse readily in sign language.

Even those who moved into the area as adults (generally after marrying into an old up-Island family), took the trouble to learn the language. One woman, now in her middle seventies, who married a man from Chilmark in the late 1920s, told me, "I learned sign language in Chilmark after I was married. My husband taught it to me. He grew up in Chilmark and he knew all the deaf and dumb people. I could talk with them enough so that we could carry on a conversation." I asked if her husband had actually sat down and given her lessons in sign language. "No, he taught me . . . I don't know, just at times, you know, he would teach me different signs. It wasn't lessons or anything. It was just so I could converse with them. And I was so interested in it, because it was interesting to see them talk and I wanted to talk with them—they were my neighbors, you see."

The casual manner of learning sign language is even more evident in another interview with a woman who married into the Chilmark community in the early 1930s:

> Oh, I learned it from, um, I don't know. I suppose my introduction to it was Abigail [who was deaf], who lived next door to us. I don't think I knew it before then. I was born on the North Road, then I moved down-Island where no deaf people were still alive down there. When I got married, I moved to Chilmark. As soon as I moved to Chilmark, I started learning the language. I had to, certainly, because everybody did speak it in town—knew the language to a certain extent.

Indeed, it was assumed that everyone in town was conversant with it. The Indian town of Gay Head, although close to Chilmark, was a distinct community and did not have much regular contact with the white towns. One Gay Header, who found himself from time to time in the general store on Menemsha Creek in Chilmark, recalled recently how awkward it was to be unable to speak sign language in a community where everyone was assumed to be familiar with it. "You know, you would go down to Ernest Mayhew's store down there, I used to feel chagrined because I couldn't speak the sign language . . . I felt so dumb! They'd say things and make signs and look pleasant and God, I—it kind of embarrassed me because I couldn't understand."

Those who knew the language were expected to know it well, and pretending ignorance, even by children, was not tolerated. "Sarah, who was deaf and dumb, you know, used to babysit for our daughter, and Sarah would tell our daughter to do something. And May, our daughter, would pretend that she didn't understand the signs. And would that make Sarah mad! Boy, she'd stamp her foot, and she'd yell!"

Difficulties in Communication Hearing Islanders apparently had no difficulty in communicating with the deaf, although we cannot know with certainty. All communication was in sign language, for it seems that none of the deaf Vineyarders read lips.[3] Several informants recalled that they would occasionally have difficulty with a specific word, generally one not used in daily conversation. The hearing Islander would usually ask, in sign, for the appropriate sign. Occasionally, those who knew the manual alphabet would spell out the word, but less than half of my informants knew the manual alphabet, and only a handful recalled making much use of it. Interestingly, many of them considered the manual alphabet as "real" sign language, probably reflecting the stigma that has been attached to true sign languages up until the past two decades.

In the larger society off-Island, hearing individuals often communicate with deaf persons by written notes, but there is no indication that this was done on the Island. It is not known whether the seventeenth- and eighteenth-century Vineyard deaf people were literate. In the nineteenth century all but one deaf Vineyarder could read and write English, probably learning it as a second language in school.[4] The few surviving letters by these deaf men and women show a good command of written English.[5] Hence most of them could have written notes to communicate with hearing individuals if the need arose, but in fact, no one remembered this happening. Most informants insisted they never saw any of the deaf Vineyarders using written forms of communication. As one told me: "They never wrote anything that I could remember. Of course, I was young then, but I don't know. They always used to, you could figure out what they were going to say. You know, you were so used to it." There was only one hint that any of the deaf Vineyarders communicated in writing. One man remembered that his neighbor, a deaf woman, whose husband ran a milk and wood business that the summer people used, often kept a broken slate and a piece of chalk by her back door in case she had trouble communicating with an off-Islander.

The continual use of sign language in the up-Island communities seems to have fostered a free and easy exchange of ideas and concerns among all members of the community.

Now you see, I can't honestly remember how many [hearing people] spoke the language well and how many didn't . . . Most would have enough command of the language to understand. And to make themselves known too.

They could all read, but using sign language, you could make 'em all understand somehow. I never heard of anybody having any problem, I don't know as I ever did.

Oh, I could talk the sign language, get along with them in pretty good shape—most everybody could. I never learned the alphabet, but, ah, most individuals knew the signs.

Competency of Hearing Signers   It is, of course, possible that hearing Islanders believed they spoke sign language better than they actually did. As with any sign language, if the person signing is not adept at it, a deaf individual can miss a significant portion of what is being said. While a hearing person might go on his or her way believing the deaf individual has understood every word, this may actually not be so. During the course of my interviews I paid particular attention to this question, asking close relatives of deaf Vineyarders whether understanding hearing people was a problem. None recalled that their deaf relatives had complained about or commented on this.

A true sign language has its own unique grammar, syntax, and idiomatic structure. Some hearing Vineyarders may have used a pidgin sign system—fitting signs into an English grammatical structure, with a heavy dose of finger spelling by those who knew the manual alphabet. Some may have spoken a pidgin sign language but understood the Vineyard sign language when it was used, since the ability to comprehend is often more developed than the ability to speak correctly. Off-Island, pidgin sign languages are the most usual form of manual communication used by hearing adults (Woodward 1973a; Woodward and Markowicz 1975; Bronstein 1978).

Hearing adults who learn sign language are usually influenced by the grammatical forms of their spoken first language, but hearing Vineyarders may have been less influenced by this, for they generally learned sign language in very early childhood. Many informants remembered that the word order of sign language was different from that in English, and many noted that one sign would say "many different things." "Those of us up here who had contact with these people on a regular basis, we could speak it faster and, well, we could abbreviate a lot of things, you know, one word might mean a whole sentence."

A number of informants also insisted that there was no difference in the types of signs or their order when used by deaf Islanders talking among themselves and by hearing individuals with the deaf. This is significant, for some deaf signers off-Island, when speaking to a hearing person, will switch into signed English (a more or less word-by-word translation of English into signs), rather than use American Sign Language (Markowicz and Woodward 1978). On the Island, however, the only distinction made was that when talking to a hearing person who was not very fluent in the language, "like with someone who would not have day-to-day contact with them," the deaf person would sign more slowly.

Sign Language in Daily Life   The community's bilingualism extended into every facet of daily life. Sign language formed an integral part of all communicative events. All informants remembered the deaf Vineyarders participating freely in discussions.

> When I used to go up to Chilmark, there were several people there who were deaf and dumb, there were so many of them that nobody thought anything about it, but because I was only a boy, I was fascinated watching them and then I was wondering what they were saying. And they would have, when they had socials or anything up in Chilmark, why, everybody would go and they [the deaf] enjoyed it, just as much as anybody did. They used to have fun—we all did.

Another remembered, "Well, wherever we met, they'd go to most everything that we'd go to around town. And in the office there in Chilmark, we went to get our mail there most days, so we'd all meet there."

As in many small New England towns, in Chilmark the combination general store and post office was a focal point for stories, news, and gossip. In the summer people gathered on the front porch, in the winter, around the pot-bellied stove. Many people I talked to distinctly remembered the deaf members of the community in this situation. One man in his late eighties recalled:

We would sit around and wait for the mail to come in and just talk. And the deaf would be there, everyone would be there. And they were part of the crowd, and they were accepted. They were fishermen and farmers and everything else. And they wanted to find out the news just as much as the rest of us. And oftentimes people would tell stories and make signs at the same time so everyone could follow him together. Of course, sometimes, if there were more deaf than hearing there, everyone would speak sign language—just to be polite, you know.

Another man said, "If there were several people present and there was a deaf man or woman in the crowd, he'd take upon himself the discussion of anything, jokes or news or anything like that. They were always part of it, they were never excluded."

His wife remembered:

You'd go along and get your mail, or you'd buy half a pound of salt pork . . . They'd gather every night. There'd be conversations going on between these deaf people, some of them are talking, making sign language, some of them are talking to hearing people, back and forth, and it was give and take. You never thought anything about it. And even these little kids . . . knew the sign language. And these older men would stop and talk to them kids, make signs back and forth, laugh and chuckle."

Another remembered:

I learned it when I was a kid. Everybody in town knew it. Yeah, these men and women, mostly men, would be at the post office every night. There'd be six or eight of 'em, and they'd be no different than you or I. They'd mingle in with everybody—everybody knew the language. Everybody talked with 'em—just like you'd do to a person who could speak.

When they assembled right before the mail in Chilmark, for example, at night, and there would be deaf mutes there, and there would be plenty of people who could talk and hear, and they were all part of the crowd. They had no trouble, no trouble at all.

The sign language sometimes proved disconcerting to visitors who wandered into the Chilmark general store. One woman from Vineyard

Haven recalled going camping up-Island as a child with her family near the turn of the century. By that time, no deaf individuals were still alive down-Island, so a young child would rarely have seen individuals speaking in signs.

> That was the general store, the Chilmark general store. And we used to walk through the woods to go over there very often to telephone and get our mail, you see . . . There were all these people sitting around the store, you know, at night, the way it is with country stores. People gathered, it's a regular gathering place, social occasion. And there were several men and one young woman, there was no noise, there wasn't a sound, but they kept smiling and chuckling, so we were very much surprised and finally we realized that they were deaf and dumb. It must of been, must of been ten of them, I guess.

At least these down-Islanders were aware that deaf people lived up-Island, and they were able to piece together what was going on. But the whole town had a good laugh over the story of one summer visitor.

> Well, there was a man by the name of Joseph Walenski, who was a famous artist. I don't like his art work, but he was . . . And he came into the store one night, the post office was open as long as the store was, to buy a stamp and mail a letter. That was the meeting place for everybody in town, the deaf and dumb as well as those who weren't and, of course, everybody used the sign language, and they'd be making the signs in sign language. There would be a complete silence in there, and even those who could talk would often be silent.
>
> And Joseph Walenski walked in there one night, there was this assemblage of great big men, they were big, and there was complete silence, and the place was only lighted by the kerosene lamps, you know. And there were these tremendously big men—dim in the store, dim light—standing around, perfectly silent, looking at him. And he thought [they looked] aggressive. But of course they weren't, they were just, you know, making signs among themselves. He was scared to death.

I asked if all the men present that night were deaf. "Oh no, only four of them were."

Sign language was also used in larger groups. One man told me:

> They would come to prayer meetings; most all of them were
> regular church people, you know. They would come when people
> offered testimonials, and they would get up in front of the audi-
> ence and stand there and give a whole lecture in sign. No one
> translated it to the audience because everyone knew what they
> were saying. And if there was anyone who missed something,
> somewhere, somebody sitting near them would be able to tell
> them about it.

According to a brief biography of a deaf man in the *Vineyard Gazette*'s "Old Time Vineyarders" series, the only concession to deafness
at the prayer meetings was that the deaf church members were permitted to stand at the front of the room so the audience could better
see their confessions.

> An interesting demonstration of the use of sign language was
> formerly a common sight at village prayer meetings. Mr. Brewer,
> like all his family, has always been a regular attendant at religious
> services and on such occasions as prayer meetings, the members
> of his family "spoke" or offered prayers as others did. In order
> that the congregation might know what they "said," it was cus-
> tomary for them to walk to the front of the room, where they
> would offer their adoration in sign language. (*Vineyard Gazette*
> 1931)

This practice seems to have occurred regularly for many years on
the Island. A Vineyard clergyman called "Reformation" John Adams
mentioned a deaf man at a prayer meeting in 1821 (Adams 1853). An
account of one of the early Cottage City meetings noted: "Most soul-
stirring of all is to see a deaf and dumb sister speak in signs of the
goodness and wonderful works of God" (Hough 1936:40).

Several informants recalled that at town meeting a hearing person
would stand at the side of the room and translate the often lengthy
and frequently heated discussions into sign language so that all the
deaf people could follow it. Because sign language was known so
widely, no one individual was singled out as translator, although those
with deaf family members probably filled this role more often.

In fact, there was little need for translators on a day-to-day basis. Almost everyone who had even occasional contact with people from West Tisbury and Chilmark could speak "well enough to get by," including the postmaster, delivery clerks from down-Island stores, and the doctor from Vineyard Haven (a nephew of two deaf men and a grandson of two others). If someone who could not speak the language came up-Island, any nearby hearing person was pressed into service. Presumably, this was also true down-Island as well until the middle of the nineteenth century.

The only regular event for which deaf Vineyarders needed some assistance seems to have been the Sunday church sermon. Most of them attended church regularly, and a spouse or other relative usually translated. One informant remembered that the hearing wife of a deaf man "used to sit side of him in church and give him the sermon. She'd sit there and her hands were flying all the time, and he was getting every word of the sermon . . . She moved her hands just about the same as a person would if they were knitting a sock, just down in her lap." Another couple would "sit way up in front and he'd sit partly around in the pew and she'd interpret every word about the sermon. And he'd shake his head sometimes, and he'd shake his head 'no,' he didn't agree. She never missed a thing. She gave him the whole thing." An elderly woman reported:

> My son came home with a friend . . . from off-Island, who was studying for the ministry. The news got around that my son had brought home a minister, so he was . . . invited to speak in church that Sunday. And he said he would. Well, Mr. B. was deaf and dumb and he and his family always sat in one of the front pews. She'd always preach the whole sermon to him in deaf and dumb sign. So this ministry student, he preached and when we come back home, I asked him how he thought it went. "All right" he said, "except there was one lady in the front pew who was awfully nervous, couldn't keep her hands still." I explained and he thought that was wonderful, he was very flattered.

Signing by Hearing Islanders   Hearing members of the community were so accustomed to using signs that the language found its way into discussions even when no deaf people were present. Where speaking was out of place, as in church or at school, hearing people often communicated in sign. Such stories as the following were common:

> Fred and I sat across the aisle from each other in school. His grandfather was deaf, so he could talk real good, and the teacher, she was from off-Island, she'd always yell "Stop talking." If she'd of said "Stop communicating," she'd of had us there, but as it was, we'd just say, "We're not talking" and go on doing it.

> Ben and his brother could both talk and hear, but I've seen them sitting across from each other in town meetings or in church (when they were both old men), and telling each other funny stories in sign language . . . I remember the last time I ever saw Ben in one such assembly, and he was not feeling good . . . And he was telling Ernest that he wasn't feeling well, and telling how he didn't feel well, in sign language.

One woman remembered her in-laws from up-Island, who were hearing and who had no close relatives who were deaf. "They'd make the signs, or very often, they'd use a sign to say something—well, it was just kind of reflex, like scratch your head, you know. They were so in the habit of doing it. They'd transfer back and forth between speaking and sign language." Another man recalled seeing signs used "all the time, at the post office, or around the beach. I spent all my time then, as I do now, around the beach, and particularly if there was a group of men there and they were about to discuss something that was either your family affair or they didn't want to get too involved in, they'd stop talking with tongues, turn around, and make signs."

Signs were also used when distance made it impossible to be heard. One man remembered, "Jim had a shop down on the shore of Tisbury Pond, and his house was a ways away, up on the high land. When Prudy, his wife, wanted to tell Jim something, she'd come to the door, blow a fish horn, and Jim would step outside. He'd say, 'Excuse me, Prudy wants me for something,' then she'd make signs to tell him what she needed done."

Another recounted, "I have seen Jonathan and Sally, I have actually seen them on a windy day talking to each other in deaf and dumb language when they could just as well have spoken. Sally was on our side of the fence—come to see me about something—and they could of perfectly well talked, but they would of had to raise their voices." One lady recalled often seeing her hearing father standing on a windy cliff and signing his intentions to fellow fishermen on the shore below.

These practices were noted in newspapers. In the *Vineyard Gazette* (1933), a reporter who had grown up in Chilmark referred to this practice, then still current. "This sign language is often used in conversing at long distances, both by deaf-mutes and others who find it a convenience. Raising the arms until they stand out from the body or above the head, Mr. North [a deaf man], and his wife, for instance, can carry on coversations at a distance far beyond the range of the human voice."

The *Boston Sunday Herald* (1895) reported:

> Nowhere else in the world could you see such singular pantomimes as are carried on daily from Chilmark back doors. Suppose you live in a lonely farm house and your nearest neighbor is an eighth of a mile away. Your men folk in both houses are fisherfolk, and so you have spyglasses. You go to your door at eleven, say, in the morning. Your neighbor is at hers. You signal to her in the sign language with your glass some question about the catch or the take from the lobster pots or a bit of womanly gossip and then you put your glass to your eye and she waves to you with her glass her reply.

Sign language was also used by fishermen in boats on the open water. One man recalled, "Fishermen hauling pots outside in the Sound or off Gay Head, when they would be heaven knows how far apart, would discuss how the luck was running—all that sort of thing. These men could talk and hear all right, but it'd be too far to yell." Another man, originally from off-Island, remembered his first exposure to the use of sign language:

> I do know that my father-in-law and his brother [both hearing] used to converse when they'd pass in boats [in sign language]. I remember one time we were out there in the Bight, and this is when I had first started coming to Martha's Vineyard, the first or second trip. He said, "There's Zeno," and he went on to tell how

> many lobsters he had in the hold, which string was doing well,
> what wasn't, so forth and all this stuff. We were probably a hundred,
> a hundred fifty yards apart. They'd hold their hands up here
> [above their heads], where they'd be clearly seen.

One off-Island woman recalled, "One time, my husband was out on a
fishing boat, a pleasure boat with one of the regular fishermen, and
when he came in, when this fisherman came in, he made deaf and
dumb language signs to the people on the shore, to a certain man on
the shore, because he wanted him to understand how many fish he
had."

Since the Islanders turned to fishing long after sign language seems
to have come into regular use on the Vineyard, it is unlikely that the
language was developed for maritime use. Signs for boats, fishing
equipment, marine life, and so forth must have been added to the
original language. However, it seems to have been a particularly effective means of communication on the water and was regularly used
there, as well as on land.

As in other bilingual communities, use of the language was a way
to delineate who was and who was not a member of the community.
Island people frequently maintained social distance from off-Islanders
by exchanging comments about them in sign language:

> My husband had a friend, and when they were grown men, they
> were in New Bedford, getting their boats repaired—and they were
> always full of mischief. So they would get on the electrics [electric
> trolley cars] and go uptown. And just to cause trouble, one would
> sit on one end of the car and one would sit down at the other,
> and they'd make funny remarks about fellow passengers and dis-
> cuss plans. And my husband said people would look at them. I
> believe they thought they were crazy! They used to think it was
> very funny.

Two young hearing up-Island men went to visit the daughters of a
family who had come to the Vineyard for the summer.

> I believe I told you about Jonathan, going off with somebody there
> to a house over near the brick yard when they were young men,
> before they were married. The man with him made some sort of
> a sign to him in the sign language, and he made a sign back and
> these girls immediately assumed that Jonathan was deaf and dumb.

Since they'd heard that there were people down there like that, they simply assumed that he was.

Jonathan was a great character, so he and this friend carried on throughout the evening, and in the process of the evening, the girls told the friend how sorry they were for Jonathan and how handsome he was. Things like that. And they finally were ready to leave. Of course, his friend was doing all the translating by hand. When they were ready to leave, why Jonathan got his hat and coat on, and then he says: "Jeese, it was a lovely evening." He would tell that story and laugh.

Jonathan's father and grandfather were deaf. Although the girls were mistaken in assuming he was deaf, it was his initial communication in sign language that caused them to make that mistake.

What linguists call code-switching from speech to sign also seems to have occurred. I was told:

> People would start off a sentence in speaking and then finish it off in sign language, especially if they were saying something dirty. The punch line would often be in sign language. If there was a bunch of guys standing around the general store telling a [dirty] story and a woman walked in, they'd turn away from her and finish the story in sign language.

Perhaps the following anecdote best illustrates how integral sign language was to all aspects of life:

> My mother was in the New Bedford hospital—had a very serious operation. And my father went over in his boat and lived aboard his boat and went to the hospital to see her every single night. The surgeon, when he left him in her room, said they mustn't speak, father couldn't say a word to her. So he didn't. But they made signs for about half an hour, and mother got so worked up, they had to send father out, wouldn't let him stay any longer.

• Research on Sign Language

Until very recently, sign languages were considered, at best, to be derivatives of spoken languages. They were believed to be universally intelligible and largely iconic in nature. Early scholars often referred to "the" sign language and attempted to investigate its supposed universal properties by studying one particular sign language system.

One area of difficulty was that sign languages were confused with sign "systems," the gestures used by hearing people in place of spoken language, such as Plains Indian sign language, those used in some monastic orders, and the hunting language of Australian Aborigines. These substitutions are word-for-word translations of spoken language. A sign language, by comparison, is generally the first language of the person who uses it. This language differs in grammar, syntax, expression, and idiomatic usage from the spoken language used by hearing members of the same community.[6]

The Development of Sign Languages How sign languages develop is a subject that has only recently come under closer scrutiny. Only 10 percent of those born deaf have deaf parents. Although some hearing parents have deaf relatives and may themselves speak sign language, most hearing parents have no prior knowledge of deafness and are forced to develop their own systems of communications, or "home signs," to use Woodward's (1978b) term, with their isolated deaf children. A study of several of these isolated deaf children has shown that they all attempt to make gestures to communicate, with varying degrees of success, with members of their immediate family. (Goldin-Meadow and Feldman 1977; Feldman, Goldin-Meadow, and Gleitman 1978).

Kuschel (1973, 1974) studied the only deaf adult on Rennell Island in the Solomon Islands. This man, the first known deaf person to appear in twenty-four generations, invented his own sign language, with which he could communicate most daily needs and discuss major topics of interest. He never married, which was unusual for his culture, and he did not fully participate in all aspects of his society, apparently because his sign language was not complex enough to communicate fully with others, although many members of the community did learn to understand his signs to some extent. But hearing individuals rarely seem willing to learn the idiosyncratic signs of a single deaf person in their community. Most isolated deaf individuals have very little real communication with those in their immediate families and virtually none with those outside the family.

When deafness appears regularly in a community, it seems reasonable to expect that signs will arise, be systematized in some manner, and begin to form an actual language. Washabaugh, Woodward, and DeSantis (1978, 1980), working on Providence Island off the coast of Columbia, and Shuman (1980a, b) working in the Mayan village of Nohya, looked at the development of sign language in small groups that apparently have recessive hereditary deafness. On both Providence Island and in Nohya, the sign language that developed over the two generations in which deafness occurred was more complex than that of the man on Rennell Island, but it was still somewhat limited in range and complexity. For example, the Providence Island sign language was found to be heavily context dependent. In both these societies the deaf were accepted but constrained from full participation in the community because of their difficulties in communicating (Shuman 1980b). Presumably these sign language systems will become more complex if there are more deaf people in future generations. These two communities probably represent a second stage in the development of sign language.

In age and complexity of the language and extent of bilingualism, Martha's Vineyard is at the other end of the spectrum. The deaf community was twelve generations deep on the Island itself, and its Kentish antecedents may go back generations more.

The examples from Providence Island, Nohya, and Martha's Vineyard cannot be dismissed as isolated or unimportant instances of the development of sign languages. Hereditary deafness is one of the most common Mendelian traits, and disease, such as iodine deficiency, which in extreme cases results in early deafness, has been endemic in some regions for centuries. In places where deafness is not uncommon, I suggest, some form of sign language will always develop. As Schlesinger and Namir (1978) have pointed out, "Some sort of sign language has sprung up in every deaf community."

Wherever there are enough deaf people over time to systematize and pass along a language from one generation to the next, a mature, comprehensive sign language may develop. The use of signs by groups of individuals who are deaf has been described from Rennell Island, Providence Island (Washabaugh, Woodward, and DeSantis 1978, 1980), Grand Cayman Island (Washabaugh 1981), the Yucatán village of Nohya (Shuman 1980b), a group of Indian villagers in Surinam (Tervoot 1978), the Adamorable in Ghana (Frishberg 1979), and the Enga of New Guinea (Kendon 1980). People affected by iodine deficiency and goiter in the Andes and Himalayas use sign languages. Undoubtedly many more instances exist.

Travelers have rarely written about these visual forms of communication (Siger 1968), and until recently few scholars thought sign languages worthy of attention. Many of the communities in which geneticists have reported various forms of inherited deafness may prove to have sign languages of their own, which simply have not been noted by those who have done medical research in the community. How complex these languages are, how effective they are in allowing deaf individuals to express their ideas and to understand what is going on in the communities in which they live, and whether hearing individuals in these communities bother to learn these languages may depend on a number of factors. These may include the number of people in the community, the length of time in which deaf individuals have been in the population, the community status of the deaf people, and the attitude of hearing individuals toward those who are deaf. All that can be said at this point is that the appearance of deafness in an isolated community such as the Vineyard is certainly not a unique occurrence, and we need to know much more about the wide range of adaptations that communities make to this disability.

Until recently, many people believed that the sign languages used in educational institutions for the deaf in the West were relatively young, based on a French Sign Language "invented" at one of the first schools for the deaf, which was established in Paris in the 1760s.[7] It was believed that before the founding of institutions, the deaf rarely gathered together, and as institutions began only in Europe in the mid-eighteenth century, sign languages must therefore be relatively young. Tervoot, for example, wrote: "It is taken for granted here that almost nowhere do the deaf live together in such close-knit and independent groups as do some other minorities, and that they never have in early childhood an adult, fully developed linguistic system available" (1978:171).

It has frequently been assumed that sign languages have all the weaknesses of a young language: no grammatical categories or function words, few lexical items, most of them imitative or descriptive, and no syntax in the sense of spoken languages (Neuman 1968:20–21).

Another common misconception was that American Sign Language (ASL) could be traced back only to 1817, the year French Sign Language was introduced at the American School for the Deaf in Hartford. Supposedly those deaf Americans who lived before 1817 got along only on idiosyncratic sign systems. However, the linguist James Woodward has challenged this belief. He has hypothesized that French Sign Language could not have been transmuted so rapidly into a recognizably different language known as American Sign Language except by creolization with one or more established indigenous American sign languages (Woodward 1978b).[8]

The data from Martha's Vineyard clearly confirms the existence of indigenous sign languages. By 1817 deaf Vineyarders had been actively participating in Island society for well over a century. Some sort of sign language must have allowed communication between the deaf and hearing during these years. Indeed, it must have existed prior to this, because even for the first deaf Islander, Jonathan Lambert, there seems to have been no language barrier.

British Sign Language   As I noted earlier, we do have a specific reference by Pepys to the use of a sign language by Downing, who had been raised in the Weald. Research on sign languages in England unfortunately has been quite limited. For the past century the British have emphasized teaching deaf people lip reading and speech, and many scholars have had a very low opinion of sign languages. Only recently has research been done on the subject (Woll, Kyle, and Deuchan 1981). Although historical references are scarce, what little information does exist indicates that sign languages have been used in England at least as far back as the Middle Ages. Bulwer (1648), in the first book on the subject to be published in English, referred directly to deaf sign language: ". . . since you already can express your selves so truely by finger, from a habit you have gotten by using always fingers, as wee doe speech." He cited several examples of deaf manual communication, including in his survey the young deaf servant of a duke, whose "use is to declare with a marvelous readiness by gestures of his body and by motions of his fingers any new thing he seeth done in the court or city." Of two deaf sisters from Cheshire, he said, "Some Cheshire men of my acquaintance who knew them both, affirme, that they had a very strange and admirable nimbleness of perception, both to understand others, and to deliver their owne mindes by fingers."

It might be argued that these examples are of idiosyncratic sign systems known only by those persons most closely associated with the deaf individuals. Carew, however, in his *Survey of Cornwall* (1602), mentioned a more widely understood sign language.

> Edward Bone, of Landock, in this country, was servant to Mr. Courtney therein. He was deaf from his cradle, and consequently dumb, (Nature cannot give out what it hath not received,) yet could learn and express to his master any news that was stirring in the Country; . . . There was one Kempe, not living far off, defected accordingly; on whose meetings there were such embracements, such strange, often and earnest tokenings, and such hearty laughters and other passionate gestures, that their want of a tongue seemed rather an hindrance to others conceiving them, than to their conceiving one another. (*American Annals of the Deaf* 1870b:189)

Their sign language was apparently well developed. Since it was mutually intelligible, it may have been a regional language.

The medieval church permitted the deaf to marry in a "ceremony conducted in sign language" (Silverman 1970:376), which presupposes that more than one deaf person knew and used a system of mutually intelligible signs.

Sibscota, another early British scholar, mentioned in *The Deafe and Dumb Man's Discourse* that "as the mutes do by their gestures exactly and distinctly understand one another, and those Persons also that use such a kind of analogous Speech among them, so they conceive many things by Gestures ([1670] 1967:43).

Bonet, observing the deaf in his area of England in 1620, assumed that sign language was a "natural" or "universal" language, citing as proof that "when mutes happen to meet who never saw each other before, they can understand each other, using the same signs" (H. Peet 1851:202–203). In an era when travel was extremely limited, these "mutes" might have lived close by, and the "natural language" described by Bonet may well have been a shared regional sign language. Even today, English sign language is noted for its large number of dialects. As Battison and Jordan pointed out, "A standard story, told by travellers and natives alike, holds that if you travel 50 miles in Britain you will encounter a different sign language that cannot be understood in the region you have just left" (1976:59). This diversity stems in part from the fact that in schools for the deaf sign language was strictly limited or forbidden altogether, so a uniform language did not develop, but the diversity of dialects also points to a very long period of isolated regional development.

We do not yet know whether the Vineyard sign language of the nineteenth and twentieth centuries reflects a Kentish sign dialect. What is important to emphasize at this point, however, is that the sign language used on the Vineyard seems to have had a considerable time depth and thus may have been based on an English sign language.

Vineyard Sign Language in the Nineteenth Century When deaf Island children began to attend school in Hartford in the nineteenth century, the Island sign language seems to have acquired some aspects of the emerging American Sign Language. It is also possible that the Vineyard sign language influenced the development of certain aspects of American Sign Language. It may have been one of the established indigenous languages that, as Woodward believes, affected the transition from French Sign Language. Verifying this statement will require a great deal of additional research, but certain facts are most interesting.

For the first several decades after the founding of the American Asylum (the same decades in which French Sign Language, introduced to America in 1817, changed so drastically), the single largest group of deaf children seems to have been from Martha's Vineyard (*American Annals of the Deaf* 1852). No other area sent anywhere near so many children to Hartford, and most of the other students had grown up in small towns and rural areas, knowing few or no other deaf children (Clerc 1818).

Also, the second largest group of students over the years (children who came from the same area and were in some cases related) was from the Sandy River area of Maine. These children were descendants of the people who had emigrated from Martha's Vineyard less than a generation earlier. Their parents had stayed in contact with the Island in the intervening years, and it is likely that the sign language used in Maine was similar to that used by the Vineyarders.

The Vineyard language, as remembered by my informants, resembled American Sign Language in many ways. The reason may not be

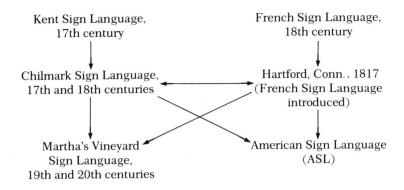

just that the two languages were creolized, but also that some features of ASL were taken from the Vineyard language. Schematically, this development would look as shown in the figure above.

In any case, the original sign language used on the Vineyard does seem to have acquired many characteristics of the more widely used ASL as increasing numbers of deaf Island children were sent to the American Asylum in Hartford after 1850. The resulting creolized sign language was in many ways unique to Martha's Vineyard. My informants remembered signs for many specific words that were different from the ASL signs, and Islanders who recalled the language commonly said that they found it very difficult or impossible to understand the sign language spoken by deaf off-Islanders or the occasional translations for the deaf on television.

• • • • • • • • • • • • • • • •

6

Growing Up Deaf on the Vineyard

How would a bilingual community—in which "every resident . . . learns to talk with fingers as early as with his tongue, for he will have to do with the deaf socially and in business every day and every hour of the day" *(Boston Sunday Herald* 1895)—actually function on a daily basis?

The widespread use of sign language affected every aspect of Vineyard society. It was not simply a question of language usage; the attitude of hearing people toward the deaf and their ability to communicate easily and well extended into every aspect of Vineyard society. There was no language barrier and, by extension, there seems to have been no social barrier.

Recent research indicates that deaf children of deaf parents fare better both socially and academically than deaf children of hearing parents who do not sign (Meadow 1968; Schlesinger and Meadow 1972; Nash 1981). The deaf parents' acceptance of the child's deafness, the ability to communicate through sign language, the availability of role models, the support of the surrounding deaf community, and the knowledge of how to manage day-to-day problems are all cited as factors in this advantage. Particularly important is the head start these deaf children receive in the first few years of life. Those early years are often a difficult time for deaf children of hearing parents, as their mothers and fathers come to grips with their child's disability, struggle to master sign language, and find their way through a complicated special education system.

These difficulties were not present for deaf children on the Vineyard.

In a very real sense, the society functioned as an extended "deaf family." A hearing couple who gave birth to a deaf child knew a substantial amount about deafness. Chances were good that a close family member was deaf, and, as noted earlier, even if no one in the immediate family was deaf, almost all townspeople interacted with some deaf man, woman, or child regularly. A deaf child born into this full social acceptance began life with the same advantages as those who have deaf parents.

Although deafness is not always noted in the records except for state and federal censuses after 1830, the names of deaf individuals appear in many early Island accounts—in birth, marriage, and death records; wills; land deeds; militia rolls, and other public and private documents. These records, combined with the more recent oral history, allow us to assemble an overview of what life was like for deaf Vineyarders. Their status seems to have remained the same from the mid-seventeenth century to the twentieth, some twelve generations later.

• Childhood

Most deaf children, like their hearing counterparts, grew up in single-family households, as was usual in both England and New England (Greven 1970). On Martha's Vineyard, as elsewhere in New England, married children generally moved to a farm nearby. There was daily contact between these "nuclear" households, and family members cooperated in farming or fishing, helped out with child care, shared extra produce from the garden or the sea, borrowed tools, clothing, or equipment, and traded recipes, news, and gossip. Probably 98 percent of all Island families had at least one close family member living within walking distance. This settlement pattern was a very stable one. Although individual members of a family might move, the extended families, as well as neighborhoods made up of clusters of families, continued from one generation to the next, from one century to another.

As noted above, this exceedingly stable population was a major factor in the successful adjustment of deaf children. In a community already familiar with deafness, the appearance of a new deaf child was not cause for special concern or alarm. And the widespread knowledge of sign language made it possible for the deaf child to begin to communicate with everyone he came in contact with from a very early age. For all these reasons, the childhood of a deaf Vineyarder seems to have been much the same as for a hearing child. I heard no stories from my Island informants about these young deaf boys and girls; apparently there was nothing unusual to tell.

• Education

It is not known whether the deaf Vineyarders of the seventeenth and eighteenth centuries attended school. Public schools were instituted on the Vineyard within a few years of the first settlement, but only a handful of attendance lists survive. No names of children known to have been deaf appear on them, but that can hardly be taken as proof that they did not attend.

The signatures of deaf people on early wills, deeds, and other documents provide evidence that many of them could sign their names, and we can assume that they were at least partially literate. For many Islanders, hearing and deaf, in this period, literacy meant little more than the ability to write one's name and puzzle out phrases from the Bible.

In 1817 the first school for the deaf, the American Asylum for the Deaf and Dumb, opened in Hartford. Considered at the time the "state of the art" in deaf education, the school elicited a great deal of attention nationwide among the general hearing public as well as the deaf community. Going to study there was considered a rare educational opportunity, and after 1817 all but one of the Vineyard deaf attended the Hartford school for some period of time, usually leaving home at the age of nine or ten to spend several winters in Connecticut. Instruction at Hartford at first was primarily in sign language and later changed to the combined method. Even after the first "oral schools," which stressed lip reading for the deaf, were introduced in the 1860s, Hartford remained the alma mater for all Vineyarders. As the writer for the *Boston Sunday Herald* (1895) indicated, the Hartford school became an Island tradition:

> There has never been any attempt made to send any of the congenitally deaf children to oral schools. The feeling, in fact, is so strong in favor of the prevalence of a non-speaking race that any one who should go there and offer by the use of some magician's

wand to wipe out the affliction from the place and to prevent its recurrence, would almost be regarded as a public enemy and not as a benefactor.

The recommended period of instruction at Hartford was five years (American Asylum 1837), but education was available to deaf students in Massachusetts for up to ten years, regardless of the parents' ability to pay (Bell 1892). Almost all of the Massachusetts residents at the school, including virtually all of the Vineyarders, were funded by the state. As a result, many of the deaf Vineyarders were better educated than their hearing neighbors.

Martha's Vineyard was a relatively poor island. Even though education was highly valued, many children had to leave school by the age of ten or twelve to help at home or at sea. In the nineteenth century, rates of illiteracy and semiliteracy were high. The deaf children who received state tuition assistance were in many cases able to spend several years longer at school than their hearing siblings and friends. One man recalled, "The deaf—all of them that I can remember—they could read and they could write. They had more than the average amount of education, more than usual, and were considered well educated—which they were for the times." Several informants remembered that some of the less educated hearing people would occasionally bring a newspaper or legal document to their deaf neighbors to have it explained.

By way of comparison, it is estimated that only 25 to 35 percent of deaf Americans were literate in the nineteenth century (Gordon 1892), and many of those were only partially literate. Estimates varied widely, but at least 30 percent and possibly 75 percent of all deaf children never went to school at all.[1] Even today, although the vast majority of deaf individuals receive an education, it is estimated that many deaf children leave school with only a fourth- or fifth-grade education because of delays in learning to communicate and disruptions in special education programs (Schein and Delk 1974; Trybust and Karchmer 1977; Neisser 1983).

• Marriage

Deaf people on Martha's Vineyard married freely; about 80 percent of those who lived to marriageable age did marry, a rate very similar to that of hearing people on the Island. It is, however, strikingly high compared to the statistics on deaf marriages for the whole country, which stood at 45 percent throughout much of the nineteenth century (Fay 1898; Bell 1969). It is high even when compared to the rate for deaf Americans today.

On the Vineyard 73 percent of the deaf people born before 1817 married; of these, only 35 percent married other deaf people, compared to a national average in the late nineteenth century that was closer to 79 percent (Fay 1898).[2] Schein and Delk (1974) estimate that in 80 percent of American deaf marriages today both partners are deaf, and in another 7 percent the spouse is hard of hearing. Undoubtedly, the bilingualism of the community made marriages between hearing and deaf members more common than it was off-Island.

Deaf Vineyarders also married younger than their off-Island deaf contemporaries, who generally waited until their late twenties (Bell 1892; Fay 1898) and still do today (Schein and Delk 1974). On the Island, deaf men married at twenty-two on average, and women at twenty, virtually the same ages as hearing Islanders. Nor was the rate of remarriage on the Island in any way usual for the deaf. After the death of a spouse, most deaf people remarried; few remained single for more than a year or two except if widowed in old age. Second and third and even fourth marriages were all known; the deaf Islanders apparently had no difficulty finding a new mate.

In the seventeenth and eighteenth centuries, divorce was extremely rare, and only a handful of Islanders, none of them deaf, were divorced during this time. In the late nineteenth century, when divorce was still rare and often considered scandalous, two deaf couples were divorced on the Island. Among deaf couples on the mainland, for whom the social and economic pressures of deafness placed additional strains on marriage, the divorce rate was much higher (Fay 1898).

• Families

Throughout the history of the Island, fertility rates were exceptionally high. The only statistics for comparing the number of children born to hearing and deaf couples come from the mid- to late nineteenth century. At that time married couples in Massachusetts had on average 4.11 children (Fay 1898); Vineyard couples in the same period had an average of 6.1 children. Deaf Islanders had an average of 5.9 children, very slightly lower than the Vineyard average, but not a statistically significant difference, given the small size of the population.

The number of children born to deaf parents was also strikingly higher than the nationwide average for the deaf. In the 1880s, for example, probably because of later marriages and financial constraints, the average deaf-hearing couple had only 2.6 children (Fay 1898), half the national average. This average was slightly lower when both partners were deaf. Even in the latter twentieth century, the birth rate for both deaf-deaf and deaf-hearing couples continues to be lower than the rate for hearing couples (Schein and Delk 1974). On the Vineyard there was no statistical difference in the number of offspring born to deaf-deaf and to deaf-hearing marriages.

Social factors undoubtedly contributed to the higher fertility rates for deaf Islanders. Because the deaf were completely integrated into the community, they were in a good position both socially and economically to marry earlier than deaf people off-Island (Bell 1892) and to support a larger family.

• Making a Living

How deaf individuals supported themselves and their families, and their success in doing so, is also significant. As in other aspects of Vineyard life, there was no apparent difference between the hearing and the deaf, even for the first deaf person on the Island.

Before and after he came to the Vineyard in 1692, Jonathan Lambert worked as a carpenter and farmer and possibly as a cooper (cooper's and joiner's tools were listed in his will). A Jonathan Lambert, almost certainly the same man, was listed as serving as "master" of the brigantine *Tyral* when it was dispatched to Quebec to bring back prisoners from the famous Quebec expedition begun in 1690 (Banks 1966:297). This same Jonathan Lambert was credited with service in that military campaign and received the reward given to those who participated.

On May 17, 1694, Lambert bought a tract of Vineyard land, paying seven pounds to the local Indian sachem for sixty acres on the water in Tisbury (Banks 1966). Ever since, this area has been known as Lambert's Cove (E. Mayhew 1956:131).

There is little in any official record concerning this quiet, prosperous newcomer. At a time when most of the town and county records concerned court suits, this carpenter was notable for his ability to stay out of litigation with his neighbors. Lambert died at the age of eighty, and his will was probated the following fall. By Island standards he died a fairly wealthy man. Besides a house and land, wearing apparel, and tools, his will mentioned three "fine feather beds," three oxen, five cows, horses, swine, sheep and lambs, a sword and a gun, linen, and iron and brass objects. Books are listed in the inventory, indicating that Lambert may have been literate.[3] He gave half his house to two of his sons, and the other half was reserved for the use of his two unmarried deaf children, Beulah and Ebenezar, until they "dye and have done with it." (Such provisions were commonly made for unmarried adult children.) There is no indication in Lambert's will or in any of the accompanying papers that his deafness at all interfered with the execution of his legal rights. To serve as the master of a vessel, to marry, to raise a large family and rise to a respected position in the community—all indicate that Lambert functioned effectively in Barnstable and Vineyard society.

Lambert's career was not dissimilar to that of many other Vineyarders, both hearing and deaf, who would follow over the next two centuries. The economy of Martha's Vineyard, particularly of the up-Island towns, was based primarily on fishing and farming. Census records from Tisbury and Chilmark provide a good overview of the occupations within these communities. In the 1840 census of Tisbury, most adult males (those over fifteen) were listed as working either in navigation or agriculture. Several dozen were listed in various manufacturing and trade occupations. (Only three out of the three hundred twenty men in town were in commerce; they ran the general store). A federal census taken in Chilmark a decade later showed practically the same trades listed, this time with farmers slightly outnumbering mariners.

These listings are somewhat misleading, because most farmers also fished to some extent, and every fisherman had at least a subsistence farm. Farming families on the island raised most of their own food. When they married, the young men, both hearing and deaf, generally bought or leased farms of their own. All of the deaf men who married apparently owned their own farms. A few specialized; Nathaniel Mann had a large dairy herd and sold milk to all his neighbors; Silas Brewer grew vegetables for sale. Most maintained farms similar to the one

described in an article about Mr. North, who was deaf, which appeared
in the *Vineyard Gazette* (1931).

> Mr. North was born on a farm, the same farm upon which he
> lives today, and here he has spent his life, for his learning was
> all towards the raising of stock and agriculture, and throughout
> the vigorous years of his life he has cultivated his fields and tended
> his cattle and sheep. As a farmer his efforts have generally been
> successful, and great crops have filled the old-fashioned barn each
> autumn time.

Several informants recalled the farm of one-handed Jedidiah, who
was born deaf.

> Well, all I know of them, they were farming, they raised a lot. In
> those days, you know, they raised pretty near everything they ate.
> They had big farms, they raised a lot of things . . . He always had
> a big farm and he worked the farm and he had cattle and horses.

> One-armed Jedidiah . . . had a pasture . . . it was a beautiful pas-
> ture and he had a horse. Everybody in those days had a horse
> and a cow and some had a yoke of oxen besides. And in the
> afternoon, early evening, if the cow hadn't already shown up at
> the barn, he'd go out and yell for the cow. And you could hear
> that all over Quitsa.

This man, Jedidiah, who was reputed to be one of the best boatmen
and the best shot in Chilmark, also was remembered as the inventor
of a "muskrat trap that was so effective, they outlawed it."

For the up-Islanders, fishing was generally dory fishing. The dories
were large, beautifully designed, one-man open rowing boats. The
Vineyard waters are exceptionally rich in fish and within easy reach
of the east coast markets, so Vineyard men in the nineteenth century
could make a good living by fishing. Many of the deaf men are remembered as having been fishermen or in related trades. My informants did not remember anything about these men that was different
from their hearing contemporaries. An elderly captain said, "As I recall
it, Jonathan North operated a set of traps or fish seine in Menemsha
Bight, just north of the creek itself and [was] most successful at it."
And a retired fisherman recalled:

Josiah Brewer had a little boat, a nice little boat, and he went eeling in the ponds. And eels were a very valuable fish in those days, they were sold in New York. Buyers would come in the fall and buy them . . . and he was a very successful eeler—eel fisherman. And he also went off the beach at Squibnocket in a dory just the way the other fishermen did and went cod fishing. But he wasn't a full-time fisherman, he had a farm.

The sea claimed the lives of a number of deaf Islanders. In an article in the *Cottage City Star* of September 1881, the following accident was reported:

> One of the saddest drowning accidents for many years occurred off Gay Head on Friday last. Two brothers, Zeno and Samuel E., started about 12:00 in one of our staunch Vineyard fishing boats, from Menemsha Creek for the Island of Nomans Land. Saturday morning Mr. Clarence Cleveland was hauling lobster pots when he discovered an overturned boat floating in the sound near Dogfish bar. He immediately returned to Lobsterville, and summoned an investigating party, which visited the locality of the accident. One party discovered Mr. E.'s boat near the bar, while the land party discovered the bodies of the brothers washing in the swash on the beach near Sandy Point.
>
> Mr. Zeno E. was a deaf mute 59 years of age, and leaves a wife and one son. Mr. Samuel E. was aged 54, and leaves a wife and two sons. This is one of the saddest cases of sudden death that has occurred on our island for several years, and the afflicted mourners will have the heartfelt sympathy of the whole island in this their sudden and sad affliction.

And the Reverend Joseph Thaxter noted in his journal in September 1801 that "George Corliss Potter, the deaf and dumb son of William P., fell overboard and drowned in the English Channel, ae. 32." Benjamin E., who was deaf, and his hearing brother were lost bringing lumber over to the Island on a barge that sailed from New Bedford in the spring of 1805. He was survived by his deaf wife and two deaf sons.

The one maritime trade in which the deaf apparently did not participate was whaling. Although Edgartown was a leading whaling port, many young Island men chose not to go on such voyages, and there is no evidence that deafness was a restriction.

Almost all Vineyard men also did occasional odd jobs, such as chopping wood, building a stone wall, or haying, to help make ends meet. The deaf Islanders were no exception. Jonathan Lambert farmed and did carpentry; William Everett in the nineteenth century is recorded as having been a fisherman and a shipwright. Roy North was remembered as "having a small farm and selling firewood to half of Chilmark." One-armed Jedidiah added to his income by supplying his neighbors with game birds.

On Nomans Land, where the boats had to be hauled out of the water every evening, Ezra Brewer made a good living by hauling boats with his pair of oxen. Each boat owner paid him five dollars a season, and that, combined with his subsistence farm, was his support. Brewer also acted as a lookout for ship's pilots on Nomans Land. The pilots, who guided ships into harbor, would wait in huts on the island. Ezra would be paid to sit on a hilltop and keep a sharp eye out for inbound whaling vessels. As soon as he spotted one he would run down to get the pilot who was employing him. The pilot would race to launch his boat in hopes of reaching the vessel before the others.

Women generally did not work outside the home and farm. But many, especially spinsters or widows, took on jobs such as sewing, housekeeping, babysitting, or fancy ironing to help make ends meet. Deaf women are known to have worked at all of these jobs; two, one in the eighteenth century and one in the nineteenth, are specifically referred to as seamstresses. One may have had a small dressmaking shop in a shed behind her home.

A long-time summer person mentioned, "I was told that at one time both the minister and the local storekeeper were deaf and dumb," but this informant did not recall if he had been told specific names. No oral or written accounts mention a deaf minister or storekeeper. Perhaps summer visitors told this story to illustrate how common deafness was and how matter-of-factly it was treated by the local populace.

• Economic Success

Deaf Islanders ran the gambit of financial success from very poor to comfortable, and one man, Nathaniel Mann, was reputed to have been the richest man in Chilmark in his day. Tax and census records, statements of bank investments and land holdings give the impression that the deaf did just as well financially as hearing people. Their tax returns and statements of personal assets were no different from those of other Islanders, year in and year out. Almost all of the deaf people were neither wealthy nor impoverished but fell into that broad category of middle class.

A few of the deaf men and women who were wealthy by Vineyard standards had inherited their money. But most prospered by old-fashioned Yankee perseverance and frugality. Nathaniel Mann was born to deaf parents of modest means. His father died when he was still an infant, and his mother's resources were soon depleted. As an adult, Mann was a fisherman and a dairy farmer. At the time of his death in 1924, he had accumulated a vast land holding in Chilmark and was reputed to be worth over a quarter of a million dollars. His deaf brother, one-armed Jedidiah, was considered reasonably well-to-do, but by no means as wealthy as Nathaniel.

Several deaf individuals had trouble making ends meet, especially widows and the elderly who were in poor health. They all had been self-supporting until old age, poor health, or some calamity wiped out their savings or curtailed their ability to work. No deaf individuals were listed on the rolls of the town poor farm.

In contrast to Martha's Vineyard, in the country as a whole deaf people were not well off financially. In the nineteenth century, although some deaf Americans learned a profession, typically typesetting or mechanics, most deaf people earned substantially less, on average, than the hearing, and a disproportionate number had menial jobs (Gallaudet 1892; Fay 1898). The same is true for deaf Americans today; men earn on average 30 percent less, and women 40 percent less, than hearing people.

• Town Affairs

The laws of the United States and the Commonwealth of Massachusetts did not deny deaf adults the right to participate in town affairs, to hold office, or to vote. But in the nineteenth century and earlier, this was a moot point in most towns and cities because the prevailing attitude was that the deaf should not participate. On the Vineyard no such barriers existed. The deaf were active in town government and the local militia. Apparently all adult deaf males were allowed to vote and to hold public office, and some seem to have been quite involved in local politics. Several held town office—fence viewer, school committee member, or surveyor of highways—and were regularly returned to office. Several deaf men over the years were appointed or elected to the town board that managed the poor farm. There is no mention in any town records of a deaf man serving on the Board of Selectmen (the governing board of the town). But the same selectmen were commonly returned to office for fifteen or twenty years in a row, so few men, hearing or deaf, had a chance to serve in that capacity.

Names of deaf individuals were listed in all kinds of town records, from land deeds to records of the buying and selling of sheep crop marks (the notches cut into the ears of sheep to show ownership). Their names also appeared on petitions, from a request to the General Court of Massachusetts for protection during the Revolutionary War to a request that the legislature build a bridge across Lagoon Pond a century later.

Names of deaf individuals were also regularly included on up-Island militia rolls. Except for the first deaf Vineyarder's participation in the Quebec expedition, it is not known whether any of them actually served in the army in time of war. Vineyarders have a long history of coming to the defense of their country, but usually as merchant men or privateers, and those participants were not well recorded.

• Legal Responsibilities

From 1694, when Jonathan Lambert bought his first tract of land on the Vineyard, to 1952, when the last deaf Islander died, all but one of the Island deaf were considered fully responsible for and capable of looking after their legal affairs. They bought land, signed contracts, and made depositions and wills in their own names. The only deaf man who was considered incapable is also significant as a further illustration of the community attitude toward the deaf. This man was born on Nomans Land in 1821, one of two deaf children of a hearing mother and father. He seems to have had some mental problems. As a local historian wrote, "He . . . was a most eccentric character, well-known to fishermen as he tramped over the island with a stake in his hand and a rope tied around his waist" (Norton genealogical file). Another man recalled, "When he got along in years, middle-aged he was, he had a coffin put in his bedroom right up at the foot of the bed. He lived to be, well, in his late eighties, I think, and the first thing he saw in the morning, every single morning, and the last thing he saw at night was that coffin. It sort of reminded him that man was not immortal." Despite his unusual habits, this man maintained himself adequately for years, but when his father died in 1882, he was suddenly responsible for a large share of his parents' estate. His family did not consider him up to the responsibility and appealed to the courts to have guardians appointed for him. The appeal describe him as ". . . a Deaf-mute, uneducated, incapable of writing his own name, and in our opinion also incapable of transacting any financial business." The judge responded by declaring him legally insane. Among those signing the petition to have this man ruled insane was a nearby deaf neighbor. And one of those who was appointed his guardian was his successful older brother, also deaf.

• Social Life

The social aspects of day-to-day life on the Vineyard provide a feeling of what life was like for the deaf in these communities. Hearing and deaf people intermingled everywhere—at home, at the general store, at church, at parties. Participation by deaf family, friends, and neighbors was a normal part of everyday life.

A Vineyard student at the American Asylum in Hartford in 1861 wrote of her memories of home, and the directors included her essay in the Asylum's annual report that year, to show the progress in writing skills made by a "girl 16 years old, born deaf, under instruction four and a half years." Her piece, entitled "About a Picnic," described a traditional Vineyard clambake. It could have been written by any child who grew up on Martha's Vineyard, hearing or deaf.

> When I was a little girl, I guess I was about seven or eight years of age . . . my mother told me about the Picnic and I was very glad to go with my mother, my little brothers Samuel, George, and Daniel, but Daniel was a very little boy. Then we changed our clothes and put on our best clothes, I wore a pink dress. Then

my mother presented two or three cakes to my two brothers and me but I forgot about the cakes. It was a very pleasant afternoon and we took a very good walk up a hill and went down a hill into the woods and saw my cousins and friends sitting down to wait for us and others but some others stood up by the trees or walked pleasantly among them. I saw there was a long table placed on the ground that was bordered round by the trees and there it was very cool. Then we put our sweet cakes on the long table and there were many kinds of cakes, pies, oranges, cherries, lemonade, and beautiful flowers in glasses on it. I played with some girls and boys on the hill for pleasure. Some of the children told me about the clams in the ground and we ran to a place where clams were baked for the people to eat . . . I guess that it was about three or four o'clock when the clams were brought to the long table and all the persons and I sat down at the long table and ate the clams very well, then we ate the cakes and other things. When we had done we all walked pleasantly to the sea to look at it for a little while or talked to each other and we had an excellent Picnic. (American Asylum 1861:39)

One of my informants recalled making neighborly visits:

I can remember going up there, or my husband would meet with Abigail and Sarah [two of the last of the deaf Vineyarders]. And very often, they'd drop in on Sunday afternoon at my mother-in-law's when we were all up-Island, you know. And they would talk away [in signs]. They used to ride around the Island, and they'd stop in.

One man recalled evenings at home with his aunt and her deaf husband. "When we were older, I used to go up there perhaps of an evening with my folks. And everybody [would be] talking and the jokes and so forth, and my aunt, she'd be telling things and he'd be laughing. He would be right into it, my uncle would." Another fondly recalled her deaf neighbor, who died long ago. "They used to live right next door to where my father lived. I used to go there and she used to come up to my house quite a little and talk with me. Make signs . . . just neighborly visits."

Most people's memories of the deaf centered around events that had little or nothing to do with their inability to hear: "[When we were young girls] one time we decided to walk to the general store by the road . . . And along came Mr. Jeremiah North with his horse and wagon, and he stopped for us and we got aboard. He was a nice old man. I believe, yes, that's right, he was deaf too."

One Islander recalled a deaf man in Chilmark who was involved in the time-honored Yankee practice of horse trading:

> We tried to sell a horse one time to [Eben] who lived up near Zeke Mayhew's big house up toward Gay Head, and he was talking about the horse and he looked at it. And these experts know horses, and [he] looked at the space between the hip bone and did this [holding his hands out in front of his body, indicating great width and making a vigorous chewing motion], meaning the horse eats a lot. And that was true—couldn't get any flesh off that horse, the horse was always skinny.

A man who is now nearly ninety remembered that what had impressed him most about Obed Parker, an elderly deaf man who died shortly after the turn of the century, was the thing guaranteed to impress any Vineyard boy of his age—his boat:

> When I was about fourteen years old, Mr. Parker, he had a Nomansland boat, a beautiful one. He painted her all up and had an engine put in it. And I went down to the shed which was there on the east side of Menemsha Creek at that time. He had the boat in there and he was painting it. Painting the ribbon red, the hull was white with a green bottom or red bottom, and I asked him about was he going to put the mast in it. I pointed [imitates hauling of a line], and he said no, he was going to put an engine in it [makes the sign for engine, a circular movement with the right hand away from the body at chest level in a clockwise direction, suggesting the cranking of a motor].
>
> And he would go out in that thing, he had a pal down at Lambert's Cove, I don't know who he was, that he used to go and visit. And he would go down there with this boat and visit with this fellow and come back again. If that engine skipped, he had the vibrations down pat, and he would know in a minute if she was running shy of gas or something like that, and he would take

care of it. It was interesting to see. [He was a good boatman], but he was no more competent than anybody else.

Another man, who was in his early twenties at the turn of the century, recalled this same man's storytelling ability. "He was a great storyteller, despite his lack of speech. He would tell the stories in deaf and dumb, and his stories are remembered by all who knew him."

Of Eben Brewer, one person said, "I used to enjoy talking with Eben. He'd tell about going out in the garden, hoeing, and stuff coming up. Yes, he did a lot of farming." A woman recalled that when she came to the Island as a bride, she set about learning the sign language. One of her first opportunities to practice it was with old Mr. North:

> My husband had gone dory fishing off Squibnocket one time and had gotten some codfish. I was on my way out, going mayflowering, and he said that if I ran into Mr. Joshua North, I should be sure to tell him that my husband had left a big codfish for him in his boathouse. Mr. North did walk by as I was mayflowering and so I went over and said hello, and told him about the codfish in our boathouse. He said "thank you, I know about it."

A man remembered that his neighbor, an aging deaf woman, enjoyed a "nip" now and then. "She also liked her small pleasures, and on many an occasion, as my cousin and I set out on a Saturday night to do his grocery shopping in Vineyard Haven, there would come a knock on the door, and Abigail would present a five-dollar bill together with a request to purchase a pint of her favorite gin."

• Community Events

The up-Islanders had seasonal rounds of social events, and deaf members of the community were fully integrated into these affairs. One woman said, "If we had anything, everybody'd be there—oh sure." Another man was emphatic on this point. "Oh yes, yes, yes! If they had any socials or anything, they'd always go to them, and sometimes they'd have suppers, you know, chicken or chowder suppers or something, they'd always go . . . That would be at the town hall. The town hall upstairs, where the police station is now. That's where all the social functions were held."

There was always a card game or a checkers game set up in the general store:

> Oh, [you'd see the deaf] all over town. Now Eben Brewer, he loved to play cards. He was a farmer more or less, but he loved to play cards and checkers and games. Very good at games . . . very good card player. Of course, they had signs for when they were playing cards, for different suits . . . Yes, that's what we used to do, because I played cards, a good many games of cards with them over in the, well, it was the Chilmark store.

Many up-Islanders, hearing and deaf, were enthusiastic card players.

> I used to like to play whist, it's cards, you know. So they had this big card party and everybody went. So Eben Brewer and his aunt, Abigail, . . . they were partners, see—and they sat at my table with their hands a-going. And I set, I was the opposite, see. Well, I knew enough to know that they were telling each other what kinds of cards they had [laughs]. Really, I got more fun—they took all the tricks, I just hoped they'd get the first prize, 'cause it was comical. Oh, I understood them. Oh yes, sure, they knew me. He winked at me, but my partner was a summer person. I can see them now, their faces were all aglow. They were tickled to death.

Parties for young people were often given after prayer meetings, and "plum porridge" parties were quite popular. A lady whose family, from New Jersey, was one of the first to spend summers up-Island recalled the first time she met one of the Island deaf at a Tucker party.[4]

> I went to a Tucker party. We often had Tucker parties. The Methodists didn't believe in dancing, you see, so we walked around and we'd change partners and we'd face our partners and we went right and left and we went left and right and did all sorts of things like that . . . They were benefits usually, benefits for the library or the church, or something . . .
>
> And so I was talking to this little old gentleman—he wasn't awfully old, but he was much older than I was—I was in my teens. He was nodding and laughing and smiling, but he didn't

say anything. We would walk along, and he could tell by what everybody else did whether he was supposed to, you know, exchange. We went round, grasping hands this way, as we went round in a circle, face your partners, and they go this way . . . somebody called out—it was like a square dance. [And Jonathan], he did everything right. He was fine. We were walking along arm in arm and I was saying this and that to him, and he had no response. [After the dance] I said, "Who is that man? He didn't talk to me." And someone said, "Of course not, he's Jonathan North, he's deaf and dumb."

A woman from down-Island remembered seeing the up-Island deaf people once a year, at the county fair in West Tisbury. "I never saw them very often, only when they'd come to the fair, see. That's when all the old friends met, at the fair once a year." And another person from Edgartown recalled, "I remember people sitting on the porch there at the Agricultural Hall and meeting other people and just shaking hands and not saying anything."

Deaf members of the community were by no means exempt from the Island tradition of practical jokes:

I can remember when they used to haul the boats out at night on Nomans Land. Well, Ezra Brewer, who as you know, was deaf, they played a trick on him one day, just for deviltry. He would hook the boat up to the device on the ramp, giddy-up his oxen, and away he'd go. Never looked back. So they motioned him to go ahead one day, but they took the pin out of [the cleat in the boat] and put it on a log or something. When he looked back, he didn't have any boat. And boy, was he mad! I can remember that so clearly.

One of the deaf men was remembered as always "having fun":

Uncle Nathaniel had a . . . good sense of humor, and in the summertime, we used to go down to the pond there, bathing. They'd get a horse and wagon and go down to the pond. We'd come back . . . get all into dry clothes and then I'd go on the lawn and lay out in the sun and dry. I was lying there and not—I hardly knew he was around. He got a bucket of water from the old well, it was ice cold, pumped some up to take to the house. He saw me lying there, came over and dumped some of it on me. What a joke he got out of that!

Every small community has problems as well as pleasures, and the up-Island communities were no exception:

There was this one [deaf] lady, and oh, she was a mean one! I was going to trade a horse with her husband one time, and I went into the house to talk to him. She didn't want that horse traded, and boy, did she scream at me [in sign language]! The whole neighborhood still remembers that fight she had with her sister-in-law down here on the road. Her sister-in-law could hear fine, but she could sure hold her own fighting in the sign language too, I'll tell ya . . .

Another informant recalled that this same woman once burst into his kitchen and accused a member of his family of stealing her chickens. The relative was innocent, but in the ensuing argument, "She yelled at me, and I told her off, but good! Come to think of it, I guess we did our yelling in sign language."

As with all other aspects of Island life, in socializing no one made any distinctions between deaf people and hearing people. No one was able to give me an example of social activities in which only the deaf participated. Unlike the mainland, where various deaf clubs and activities are the center of social interaction for many deaf people, the Vineyard activities were attended by both the deaf and the hearing. It was not simply that the hearing Islanders welcomed the deaf into their midst; the deaf Islanders apparently made no attempt to set up activities independent of their hearing family, friends, and neighbors. If a deaf Islander wanted to entertain only other deaf individuals, he or she probably would have had to exclude spouse, siblings, children, best friends, or immediate neighbors, all of whom would have been hurt.

There were some close personal friendships between deaf Islanders, but none of them were friends exclusively or primarily with other deaf persons. Close friendships were based on whom one grew up with or who lived nearby. Nor does it seem that deaf Islanders maintained ties with deaf individuals living off-Island whom they knew from Hartford. And they did not participate in state or national deaf organizations, which are important social links for many deaf men and women on the mainland. As far as can be ascertained, deaf Islanders did not perceive themselves as a distinct social group.

• The Last Deaf Vineyarders

Early in 1952 a brief obituary in the *Vineyard Gazette* announced the passing of Mrs. Abigail Brewer: "Devoted wife and mother, active in her local church . . . will be missed by all who knew her." The article neglected to mention, no doubt because everyone knew, that she was the last member of the up-Island deaf population. In fact, the era of Vineyard deafness had begun to disappear two generations earlier.

After the turn of the century, many aspects of Island life changed. Modern conveniences, mass communication, and the influx of summer people upset many social patterns on Martha's Vineyard. One elderly Islander recalled that "in the old days" Vineyard society was somewhat stratified; families with old whaling money, the minister, the local doctor, and the other professionals were at one end of the scale. Small-time fishermen, farmers, and laborers were at the other. "When the summer people came," he said, "oh, we were all natives then."

The new people also brought an attitude toward deafness very different from the values long evident on the Island. To them, deafness was a stigma, something one should be ashamed of. At the end of the nineteenth century and into the twentieth, Vineyard deafness, especially up-Island, was occasionally mentioned in the popular and the scientific press by eugenicists as an example of the evils of inbreeding. Most of these articles were insulting to the Vineyarders, portraying them as backward, incestuous "primitives." In 1895 an article entitled "The Ascent of Man" in the magazine *The Arena* stated:

> There is a secluded hamlet on the Island of Martha's Vineyard called Chilmarth. This community, isolated from the outer, larger, pulsing world, has not only retained its primitive customs and manners, but the physical taint in the original stock has also produced a plenteous harvest of affliction.
>
> At Chilmarth the mental and physical progress is downwards, and will continue so to be until some state sanitary regulation

drives forth its male inhabitants in a modern "Rape of the Sabines."

The author concluded:

> Here is the case of a primitive people, disease tainted at the start, who go on marrying and intermarrying with disease, making no effort to introduce pure and revivifying blood. What is the inevitable result? The race becomes more and more vitiated. The octopus of affliction stretches its skinny, clammy arms every whither and enfolds an army of disease and idiocy . . .
>
> What humanity needs in many directions is prevention. They need to be prevented from reaching that condition where treatment is necessary. Prevention is the sphere and jurisdiction of government and law. (Miller 1895)

Vineyarders with deafness in their family found themselves the objects of "scientific" inquiry by summer people. A woman now in her eighties recalled:

> [When] one of my kids was a little kid, somebody came from off-Island, and wanted to come and see my child to see if she was deaf and dumb and retarded and asked my mother if they could. And I said "Go to heck! You can't come" . . . It was somebody from away. I don't know who it 'twas, don't remember. It was years and years ago, but I was so mad!

For the first time Vineyard deaf people had to contend with some of the problems faced by their off-Island counterparts. Once a new "year-round" summer person got up at town meeting to ask whether the deaf had a right to vote on issues and elections. The selectman was upset—he had never even thought about the question before. He wrote to the state attorney general, who replied, "Read your statutes." As none of the Island towns had any statutes concerning the deaf, the reply was considered a clear-cut endorsement of the deaf Islanders' right to vote. Half a century later the Islander who recounted this story still fumed that the question had been raised. Public reaction must have been very strong; the newcomer never raised the issue, or any other issue, in town meeting again.

The Islanders' opinions of summer people were lowered still further when some of them showed outright antagonism toward deaf members of the community. Two Islanders recalled the situation in the late 1920s:

> Mr. O.: Some of the newcomers couldn't understand [the sign language] too well. I can remember that R.W., who was postmaster there in Chilmark for a while . . . They made fun of them! They never even *tried* to understand any of the sign language.

> Mr. J.: Well, I know that that's true. And there were others who came—some of those people who built Windy Gates [a large estate] came from New York City, you know, round and about. And they said, "Those people ought not to be allowed to marry and bring forth children." Can you imagine that!

Some newcomers had no particular prejudice against the deaf. One of the very early up-Island vacationers, now in his late nineties, replied to my inquiry by writing:

> I spent only summer there [in Chilmark], but we did business with the Brewers [who were deaf] and others who farmed. "Sign" language was our only communication, but I saw the deaf use their own. There were only a few families, four or five . . . accepted by everybody because they performed a service as farmers—eggs and milk draw no lines. The casual acceptance of these few families did not surprise me, and I heard very infrequent references to them from their neighbors and townsmen.

Not all off-Islanders were condescending to the deaf. Many acquired some signs in order to communicate with them. The famous painter Thomas Hart Benton, who summered on the Island for years (and who was well liked by the Islanders) took pains to learn the sign language and even painted several portraits of deaf Vineyarders.

The old Island families never adopted the off-Islanders' attitude toward the deaf. Whether they would have eventually cannot be guessed at, because the number of deaf Vineyarders was so rapidly decreasing.

The deaf Islanders' participation in community life began to decline by the early 1920s. As they aged, they got around town less and became a less important and visible factor in the community. The older residents kept in touch with them, but many of the younger people, anxious to leave home for the wonders of the mainland, paid little attention to them. Few asked about them, and fewer still bothered to learn their language. The newer summer people were often not even aware of their existence.

The world was changing quickly. Deaf Ben Brewer had to be particularly careful when he drove his horses to the field.

> On the highway, where cars whiz by every other minute, Mr. B. practices safety by drawing up on the proper side of the road. The cars or vehicles approaching from in front are thus given sufficient room in which to pass. But he always knows when a vehicle is approaching from the rear. At the sound of a motor, his horse will invariably make a slight motion with its ears which Mr. B. has learned to watch for through long experience, and he turns out if necessary. (*Vineyard Gazette* 1931)

In 1923 the island of Nomans Land was sold to a summer family, and Ezra Brewer, deaf, aged, and confused, had to be dragged forcibly off the island where he had been born. He died within two years. (The navy eventually took over his island and in their infinite wisdom turned it into a combined bird sanctuary and bombing run.)

Occasionally some of the elderly deaf would be seen around town, at the general store or in church. Jeremiah North still sat around the Menemsha store, and Nathaniel Mann's wife continued to translate the sermon on Sunday. One woman recalled:

> Oh, that's a famous story in my family . . . she would, of course by that time, she was growing blind, and he was deaf and dumb, and she would hear the service. They would sit holding hands and she would talk sign language to him, repeat the whole sermon to him as they sat in church, because she could hear it. And so they were almost eyes and ears for each other, you know, toward the end of their lives.

As the older Islanders died, so too did the memories. Today Vineyard society is still distinct from that on the mainland, and from that of the summer people who throng to the island. But the importance of Martha's Vineyard as a model remains undiminished.

• • • • • • • • • • • • • • •

7

Deafness in Historical Perspective

The attitude toward deafness in Vineyard society stood in stark contrast to the prejudices and misinformation on the mainland during the same period. The experiences of deaf Islanders were significantly different from those of deaf Americans today, who continue to contend with the legacy of discrimination against them that is part of our society. Although I do not want to go into great detail here, a brief overview of deaf history will help to clarify our current attitudes toward deafness.

In 1890 Gillett stated reassuringly, "There was a time when the deaf were considered but brutes and classed as idiots, and treated accordingly. That time, all are thankful, is past; and in our time deaf persons often stand in society the peers of any other." But he saw fit to add, "There is in society a vast amount of practical ignorance concerning the deaf, which it seems almost impossible to eradicate" (Gillett 1890a:249). This "practical ignorance" seems, in fact, to have been overwhelming, as reflected in a statement by Civil War General Benjamin F. Butler, who blithely declared that "the deaf-mute is only half a man" (Gillett 1891:57).

Indeed, at times the public's attitude toward the deaf seems to have been distinctly medieval. In many places they were not allowed to assume the rights and responsibilities of adult citizens even after receiving an education (Booth 1858). And generally they were discouraged from so doing, even if not forbidden. The general view of the deaf in nineteenth-century America can perhaps best be summed up in the census tables, where "the deaf" were included in the broad and demeaning category of "defectives" (United Status Federal Census

1830–1900). Even today deaf people as a group remain isolated from the larger hearing society, both by their own choice and by the prejudice and ignorance of hearing people, who too often see deaf people as "physically, socially and linguistically pathological" (Woodward 1973a:191). This attitude is based on centuries of misinformation and misunderstanding.

Unfortunately, until very recently, little information has been available on deaf people as a group. In Western culture, history is generally written in terms of major events and famous personages; the history of "the deaf" is no exception. Although references to deaf individuals have appeared throughout written history, very little is actually known about what life was like for these people before the modern era. Only in the past two decades has serious consideration been given to the psychological and sociocultural aspects of deafness in our own society. Historical studies of deafness have generally focused on laws from Biblical, classical, and medieval times referring to deafness and on formal attempts by hearing people to teach deaf persons to speak.

Historical records indicate that the current Western attitude toward deafness is the result of a long period of development with unique and specific roots. The earliest known written mention of deafness was in the Babylonian laws, which restricted the rights of those born deaf. The next reference was in the Mosaic Code of Holiness from the sixth century B.C., which warned the faithful against cursing the deaf, presumably because many were doing just that. Four hundred years later, Talmudic rabbis imposed laws that restricted congenitally deaf individuals from assuming many of the legal rights and responsibilities of other citizens, thus placing them in the same category as children and the mentally retarded (Silverman 1970).

Hippocrates and Pliny the Elder both paid some attention to psychological aspects of deafness, particularly the difficulty in communicating. But it was the ideas of Aristotle and his contemporaries that had the farthest-reaching implications. For Aristotle, speech was the primary vehicle of thought and education. If one could not hear, one could not learn, and instruction of any sort was useless. Aristotle's beliefs about deafness were incorporated into Roman science and came to be accepted as common knowledge in the classical world (Bender 1970). As Lucretius wrote: "To instruct the deaf no art could reach / No care improve them, and no wisdom teach" (Burnet 1835:53).

In the sixth century A.D. popular beliefs about deafness were incorporated into the Justinian Code, which made a sharp distinction between those who were born deaf and those who lost their hearing after having acquired speech. The legal rights of the former group were severely curtailed (DiCarlo 1964). The Justinian Code served as a model for a number of medieval systems of law. Thus Aristotle's opinions on the link between language and intelligence was carried on into the Middle Ages, appearing virtually unchanged in both secular and church writings. Saint Augustine argued "that deafness from birth makes faith impossible, since he who is born deaf can neither hear the word nor learn it" (Seiss 1887:155).

The deaf were considered so incapable of instruction that in 685 A.D., when John of Beverly, Archbishop of York, England, taught a deaf youth to speak intelligibly, Bede referred to it as a miracle. (Others must have agreed, because it was one of the miracles that led to the archbishop's canonization.) In many places those born deaf were not permitted to marry, have a voice in government, or inherit property. The right of primogeniture, a cornerstone of inheritance in many parts of Europe was invariably denied a deaf eldest son (Scott 1870:64; Silverman 1970:376).

Most of Europe's population, of course, were peasants, who owned little property and for whom education was beyond reach. These people, often living on the verge of poverty, could hardly have allowed healthy, intellectually capable adults to do little or nothing simply because they could not hear. We have virtually no idea how these individuals communicated, what they did to earn a living, what their role in society was, or how other members of society treated them. All we know is that there must have been many deaf people.

We do know that the Enlightenment brought renewed curiosity about how the human mind worked and how language functioned. The deaf seemed to offer a potentially interesting testing ground for many theories (Puybonniex 1846). Such people as Agricola in Germany and the Italian philosopher Cardan argued that the deaf were indeed capable of instruction. These arguments were backed by a small but increasing number of attempts to educate the deaf children of wealthy families; the instructors often were prompted as much by intellectual curiosity as by compassion for the children (Seiss 1887; Silverman 1970; Savage et al. 1981).

By the middle of the seventeenth century, men of science and medicine were beginning to believe that the deaf were, in fact, capable of thought and learning (Amman 1700; Bulwer 1648; Opren 1836; Sibscota 1967). But it was still an uphill battle. John Bulwer, a contemporary of Milton and Bacon, wrote the first English treatise on deaf education. He discussed the possibility of founding a school for the deaf with some leading intellectuals of the day. He then wrote, "I soone perceived by falling into discourse with some reationall men about such a designe that the attempt seemed so paradoxicall, predigious and Hyperbolicall, that it did rather amuse than satisfie their understandings, insomuch as they tooke the tearmes and expressions this Art justly usurpes for insufferable violations of their reason" (1648:B4).

The life of the average deaf person seems to have been difficult. "The condition that they are in who are born deafe and dumbe, is indeed very sad and lamentable: for they are looked upon as misprisions in nature, and wanting speech are reckoned little better than Dumbe Animals" (Bulwer 1648:102). Amman, a Swiss physician living in Holland, began his book, published in Dutch in 1700, with the note: "Candid Reader, this art of instructing the deaf and dumb may seem to you new, and perhaps incredible" (1873:xxi).

It is interesting to note that while scholars were just beginning to address questions relating to deafness, the deaf themselves continued on unaffected. For example, when Bulwer published his book on deafness, the group of settlers from the Weald had been in Massachusetts a decade. When Amman's volume appeared, Jonathan Lambert was already married, with six children. It is highly unlikely that these books, intended for a scholarly audience, ever found their way to the Vineyard.

The eighteenth century saw the development of deaf education, capped by the establishment of schools for the deaf in the 1760s and 1770s in Paris, Leipzig, and Edinburgh.[1] But long-held prejudices were by no means quickly eliminated. The Abbé de l'Epée, founder of the school that would later become the National Institute for Deaf Mutes, and a leading figure in deaf education, found that "very respectable ecclesiastics in his own time openly condemned deaf education for theological reasons" (Mann 1836:103). The French philosopher Condillac continued to deny that the deaf had any faculty of memory and, by extension, any power of reason.

The popular opinion in America was much the same. In the nineteenth century dozens of schools and institutions were founded, but prevailing opinions about the deaf were slow to change.

It became commonplace in the nineteenth century to assume that those deaf who were not fortunate enough to be educated at a school or institution lived, as the educator Camp described it, in a "degraded condition, but little superior to that of the brute creation" (1848:214). An article in *American Annals of the Deaf and Dumb* stated:

> Between a well educated deaf mute and another of the same age who has never been under instruction, there is as wide a contrast as can well be imagined. Before going through a course of instruction and discipline, the deaf and dumb are guided almost wholly by instinct and their animal passions. They have no more opportunity of cultivating the intellect and reasoning faculties than the savages of Patagonia or the North American Indians. (1858:177)

One wonders what the deaf (as well as the Patagonians and American Indians) would have thought of such definitive statements. When this article appeared, the majority of deaf adult Americans probably had little or no education, yet many of them were competent, independent, self-supporting people, although prejudice and misinformation made it difficult to get work and often impossible to advance (Gordon 1892).

Blame should not be placed entirely on the general public's attitude toward the deaf. Educators of the deaf at times were so eager to emphasize the achievements of their students that their comparisons, between the deaf who had not had a formal education and those who had, helped fan the flames of prejudice. As Burnet insightfully pointed out, "Those who have appealed to public sympathy in behalf of the deaf and dumb have given highly coloured and, often, exaggerated pictures of this sad condition when abandoned without institution" (1835:47).

Such warnings apparently had little effect on his colleagues. Camp (1848) wrote that at the beginning of their studies, the minds of the deaf are "a perfect blank." Porter seemed to wax enthusiastic in his description of the "uneducated deaf mute";

> He is a grief and a shame to his relatives; a burden to society and when the grave hides him from the sight of the living, a sense of

relief rather than loss, fills the bosoms of those to whom nature has bound him by the closest ties . . . But with education, he becomes a new creature. Old things—the old ignorance, the old animalism, the old brutishness are passed away. (1854:15–16)

It did not take long for these ideas to be incorporated into the public's already misguided conceptions about the deaf. As Jenkins noted with disgust in 1890, "So distinguished an authority as Max Müller recently gave expression to the opinion that deaf-mutes, left to themselves, would rise no higher than orang-outangs, although he immediately qualified this by declaring himself an agnostic as to the inner life of the deaf-mutes" (1890a:185).

Even those who worked closely with the deaf were not immune from this deeply ingrained attitude. In 1870 the editor of a German journal on deafness greeted with derision the announcement that a college for the deaf (later named Gallaudet College) had been established in America:

> Having learned from a report of the Vienna Institution that such a college had been established, the editor ridicules the idea of the deaf and dumb being able to receive a collegiate, or even a high-school education, as "fast lacherlich." He compares the project to that of teaching instrumental and vocal music to deaf-mutes, and closes by saying that he will believe it possible when the blind become painters and the lame racers, when the palsied play the part of Hercules in the circus, when the deaf and dumb themselves become famous orators in churches and public halls! Meantime he borrows an English word, and declares the proposed attempt "humbug!" The director of the Vienna Institution, from whose report the editor quotes, says more prudently, and at the same time more generously, that without a close study of the pamphlet describing the inauguration of the college he would not have believed the plan feasible. (*American Annals of the Deaf and Dumb* 1870a:186–187)

Popular books and magazines featured articles on educational institutions for the deaf, considered one of the more impressive achievements of an achievement-oriented age. This did some good for the deaf community by making the public aware that the deaf could be educated, although as Mitchell noted, in schools for the deaf:

> The aim for each child was an adequate level of literacy plus knowledge by which to earn a living. Economic independence and interdependence were goals set for the deaf adult in the community, thus the instruction in manual skill or trade. The deaf person was not really expected to be part of the social community; his written English served for necessary communication with the general population, while his family and close associates could be expected to learn some sign language. (1971:349)

The eighteenth- and nineteenth-century Vineyard population was unaffected by all of this. If some Islanders were even aware of the furor in the scholarly literature and popular press over what deaf individuals were capable and incapable of doing, it seems clear that none believed it pertained to the Island or to the deaf people they knew.

Many of the problems faced by deaf Americans today have their roots in eighteenth- and nineteenth-century prejudices about deafness and those who are deaf. The gap between the rights and opportunities for hearing people and for the deaf is still large (Schein and Delk 1974; Higgins and Nash 1982). Unemployment and underemployment prohibit deaf individuals from making full use of their ideas and talents. Educational facilities and methods are slow to change, and the controversy between the oral/lipreading schools and those that teach sign language rages anew, leaving many deaf people and their families caught in the middle.

In recent years attempts have been made to break through the barrier between the deaf and the hearing worlds. A great emphasis has been placed on integrating deaf children into regular public schools and encouraging them to participate in activities with hearing children. These attempts at integration, referred to as mainstreaming, are being closely monitored by all those who work with or study deaf people. But mainstreaming affects children only; a large proportion of the adult deaf community, in both Europe and America, continues to maintain a separate identity.

This social and linguistic isolation is counterbalanced by the existence of the deaf subculture, which is distinct in many ways from the hearing culture.[2] Many deaf people consider themselves bound together by their use of sign language, shared educational experiences, high rate of endogamous marriage, and membership in deaf organizations. A growing deaf rights movement has made some inroads on the misinformation and prejudice that deaf citizens must contend with daily. A step toward fuller equality will be achieved when the society recognizes that much of what we think we know about "the deaf" and deafness is rooted in our own particular history and is not carved in stone.

• • • • • • • • • • • • • • • •

8

"Those People Weren't Handicapped"

Today, when the medical, legal, and social service professions are heatedly arguing the advantages and disadvantages of incorporating disabled individuals into mainstream society, the situation that existed on Martha's Vineyard is of particular relevance. For more than 250 years deaf Vineyarders were included and encouraged, indeed expected, to participate to the fullest extent of their ability.

It is impossible now to know exactly when or how this attitude toward deafness originated on the Vineyard. It would certainly make sense that a community that included a number of individuals who were simply unable to hear should make full use of their abilities rather than exclude them. But logic is not necessarily a strong factor in many human decisions, and we cannot attribute much to it here. Certainly many societies overlook or stigmatize their disabled members for no apparent reason; our own society is a case in point.

On the Vineyard, and presumably earlier in the Weald of Kent, the attitude toward deafness was probably the result of a unique set of historical circumstances, rather than a calculated decision arrived at by the local hearing people, who do not seem to have even regarded the deaf as a separate, recognizable group.

Two factors appear to have been essential to the adaptation to deafness evident on Martha's Vineyard. First, the trait for deafness was carried by a group of colonists, rather than by an individual or isolated family. For this reason, and because it appeared seemingly at random in the population (since it was recessive), deafness was viewed as something that could happen to any family. In fact, it did appear in most Island families at some point. The acceptance of those born deaf might not have been evident if deafness were less common.

Equally important was the use of sign language by the community, which apparently accompanied this genetic trait across the Atlantic. Just accepting the fact of deafness and treating those unable to hear with courtesy and concern does not ensure their participation in everyday life. The ease with which the first deaf Vineyarder was integrated into the population seems to indicate that a fairly sophisticated sign system was already in place. It seems logical to conclude that the language can be traced back to the Kentish Weald.

Whatever the genetic origins of Vineyard deafness, the colonists' arrival on the Island fixed and apparently intensified the original patterns. As the numbers of deaf people in the population rose with each generation, the use of sign language became universally accepted, even by those whose families were not "of Kent."

It might be argued that one reason for the success of deaf people on the Vineyard was that the Island was a small-scale, technologically simple society, where there were few tasks a deaf person was unable to do. Such a model has been formulated by Hanks and Hanks (1948), who in a general discussion of the disabled in non-Western society, suggested that individuals who are disabled have more social participation and physical protection in small-scale, relatively egalitarian societies, where group cooperation takes precedence over competition and productivity is much the same for all members. In such a situation, these authors suggested, there are few formalized criteria for evaluating success hierarchically, and the disabled are more readily accepted.

Interesting and valuable as this concept is for the study of disabilities in small-scale societies, it does not ring true for the Vineyard. Although life there did not, and still does not, run at the hectic pace found off-Island, in no stretch of the imagination could the society be considered an egalitarian one where cooperation was much more important than competition. Although always ready to be neighborly and to help, Vineyarders, hearing and deaf, were responsible for supporting themselves and their families. Paying bills, mortgages, and taxes; selling the harvest or catching fish, running for office, holding a town post or participating in old-fashioned Yankee horse trading—all these responsibilities placed deaf Vineyarders squarely in the modern competitive world. Some grew wealthy, most got by, and a few simply scraped by, just as the hearing members of their families did.

More significant, the fact that a society could adjust to disabled individuals, rather than requiring them to do all the adjusting, as is the case in American society as a whole, raises important questions about the rights of the disabled and the responsibilities of those who are not. The Martha's Vineyard experience suggests strongly that the concept of a handicap is an arbitrary social category. And if it is a question of definition, rather than a universal given, perhaps it can be redefined, and many of the cultural preconceptions summarized in the term "handicapped," as it is now used, eliminated.

The most important lesson to be learned from Martha's Vineyard is that disabled people can be full and useful members of a community if the community makes an effort to include them. The society must be willing to change slightly to adapt to all.

There is a great need for broader understanding of cultural adaptations to disabling conditions, particularly in a cross-cultural perspective. Carrying their own cultural values into the field, those scholars who study other cultures have rarely looked closely at the disabled individuals they have encountered in their work. With a few exceptions (Hanks and Hanks 1948; Edgerton 1967, 1969, 1970, 1976; Gwaltney 1970; Murphy 1976; Wilson 1974), almost all research on deviance and the disabled has been concentrated in Western Europe and North America. The bulk of it has focused on these groups in relation to some formal institutionalized setting or specific public policy.

We know relatively little about the disabled in our society and virtually nothing about them in non-Western societies. Anthropologists and sociologists have usually dismissed the disabled individuals they have encountered as liminal figures, temporary anomalies in a non-handicapped population. Many scholars, even in recent years, have not accorded any more thought to this issue than to say, for example, "Biologically handicapped children are a humanistic concern in our society, whereas in simple human populations they died early and were not missed" (Birdsell 1972:384).

But we cannot assume that those who were born or became physically impaired just disappeared from the pages of history; from 2 to

10 percent of all humanity at any given time may be disabled to some degree (Wood 1981). A significant number of sublethal and nonlethal genetic disorders are common and will reappear in a population generation after generation. Disease and accident are even more common causes of disability. The skeletal evidence in archeological records does not indicate that biologically disabled individuals inevitably died early, contributing little or nothing to the society. Nor can we assume that disabled individuals functioned only in the role of shamans or learned elders in these societies, a common explanation of why physically impaired individuals were "permitted" to live.

I suggest that the case of Martha's Vineyard may be far from unique. In communities all over the world deafness has existed and has had to be dealt with. Much more information is needed from many different types of communities before clear patterns can be shown, but Vineyard experience indicates that the hearing world's response to deafness is not always the same.

• • •

Today only a few people can remember the Island's deaf inhabitants, and fewer still can speak sign language. Some keep a few of the signs alive. As one gentleman in his late eighties told me, "You know, strangely enough, there's still vestiges of that left in some of the older families around here, I believe. Instinctively you will make some such movement, and it will mean something to you, but it doesn't mean anything to the one you're talking to." Another person mentioned, "They have gestures down here that if you, you think that the gesture is singular to one particular man, and later on you'll see somebody else doing it. I think these deaf mutes had more of an effect on this town than you realize."

But for most, the memories of the Island deaf, and of many other aspects of life on Martha's Vineyard in an earlier time, are rapidly vanishing. I began my research in 1979, and most of my informants were elderly people who had not given much thought to the Island's deaf population in several decades. Many of the facts and stories presented here could not be reassembled now, only six years later. Within two years of the beginning of this project, more than half of my informants had died.

The stories these elderly Islanders shared with me, of the deaf heritage of the Vineyard, merit careful consideration. The most striking fact about these deaf men and women is that they were *not* handicapped, because no one perceived their deafness as a handicap. As one woman said to me, "You know, we didn't think anything special about them. They were just like anyone else. When you think about it, the Island was an awfully nice place to live." Indeed it was.

Appendixes

Notes

Bibliography

Index

• • • • • • • • • • • • • • •

Oral and Written Sources

Both oral history and written records present problems that make research difficult. I cite some of these problems here.

• Written Records

Perhaps the most serious problem with written records is that they tend to be weighted toward the literate and wealthier classes. Almost all of the Vineyarders in this study were fishermen and farmers, and written accounts from and about the Island rarely mentioned such people individually. Letters, diaries, and other accounts written by the settlers themselves are even rarer, particularly from the seventeenth century and the first part of the eighteenth. Those that do exist I have used here.

The important exceptions to the lack of written records are those required by law—birth, marriage, and death certificates, censuses, and tax records, which are available for almost every inhabitant of Martha's Vineyard from the very earliest period of settlement. Unfortunately, these records are not always complete. Births were attended by local midwives rather than physicians, and a trip to the local magistrate's office to register a birth or death was often difficult and time consuming. If a child died young or if a family moved shortly after the birth, the registration of it may have been neglected. In the seventeenth century, births and deaths were generally under-recorded (Banks 1966; Lockridge 1966; Greven 1970).

One might guess that the records in a small village would be more accurate than larger towns or cities, but this is not necessarily the case. Gutman (1958) found that the record keeping in Plymouth was more lax than in larger settlements because it was assumed that everyone knew many of the details usually consigned to written documents. This was also true on the Vineyard. But there, fortunately, much of the missing information from the early years can be filled in from church records. Up until the middle of the seventeenth century, nearly everyone belonged to a church, and vital records were fairly accurately maintained.

Marriage records, particularly very early ones, also are incomplete. Generally, early and mid-seventeenth-century marriage records bore the full name of the husband and only the first name of the wife. Not until the Commonwealth of Massachusetts was formed in 1692 were clerks required to record the wife's surname (Gutman 1958), and this requirement was not strictly adhered to for another century and a half.

Because the genetic disorder discussed in this research was recessive, it is necessary to know the lineages of both the father *and* the mother in order to understand the patterns of inheritance. Unfortunately, information about women is often unobtainable, and a wife's relationships to her husband's family and to other women in her generation, whose surnames are also unknown, in many cases cannot be resolved. At best, I have mustered circumstantial evidence to help identify some of these women.

Many records have been lost over the years. In 1827 the building housing the Judicial and Probate Court and Registry of Deeds for Barnstable County burned; ninety-four volumes of information, including all the records for lower Cape Cod from the time it separated from Plymouth Plantation, were lost (Deyo 1890). The early records of many families who later moved to Martha's Vineyard were in that section. In 1861 the Chilmark town hall burned to the ground, taking with it all the early town records, except those which were fortuitously stored in the outhouse.

Church records for Chilmark prior to 1787 have simply been "lost," as have those from the ministry of John Mayhew in West Tisbury before 1689 (Banks 1966). After Mayhew's ministry there was no church and thus no church records until 1701, twelve important years later. Problems with the Tisbury records do not end there. When Nathaniel Hancock, the minister between 1727 and 1744, quit, after an "ecclesiastical quarrel," he took not only his own church records, but also the records of the previous two pastors. Hancock summarily refused to return them (Banks 1966), and they have since been lost altogether.

Names are a continual problem when tracing family ancestries; ten surnames took in most of the families on the Island, and distantly related branches of a family often named children after the same forebears. In many small settlements three or four men from different branches of a family all had identical names. Usually (but not always) the first son would be named after the father, in many cases with the same middle name. One family had sixteen generations of Benjamins. In another family Issac Norton built in the 1680s in what is now Oak Bluffs a house, which was passed down through four descendants, all named Issac (Banks 1966).

To add to the confusion, some men were named after an uncle or cousin but referred to by their families and in the legal records as "Junior." Sometimes a name skipped a generation, and a man was named Junior after a grandparent. At one point it was customary if a child died to give the next child the same name. One family had three children named Jonathan in the space of five years, and which of these was the one who was deaf is unclear. Banks noted in his genealogy of the early Vineyard settler Issac Robinson: "His son, Israel, baptized October 5, 1651, assumed the name of Issac in memory of an older half brother of that name who was drowned in 1668, and was ever after known by the adopted name" (1966, 2:61).

Although not quite so commonly as with boys, girls were often named after a mother, grandmother, or aunt. Again, the middle names were sometimes different, but confusion no doubt existed.

These naming practices were not necessarily confusing in the community, for nicknames were common, and people were often referred to by their first and middle names. But nicknames were not used on formal records and in legal documents, of course, so it can be very difficult to decide which of three of four Samuels or Mehitables or Zenos was the one who was born deaf. Those lineages that I was unable to check with certainty, I have noted in the text.

• Oral Sources

Anthropologists working with oral materials must determine the reliability of the information obtained. Whenever possible, I verified the information provided by my informants by comparing it with available written records. When oral history and written records agreed, the information was usually taken as fact. Where there was some discrepancy between the two sources, I searched further to identify the source of confusion and clarify the facts. In cases where I could not determine whether one or both sources were accurate, I have mentioned this in the text.

On the whole, the information provided by the older Islanders was highly reliable. Except for a few individuals whose memories were beginning to fade, most people's memories tallied with those of other older Islanders. No one knowingly lied, as far as I was able to determine. Some people had better memories than others, and some were more interested in the people and events around them. But on the whole, almost all of those still alive who had been members of the Island communities sixty or seventy or eighty years ago shared similar memories and attitudes. The accuracy of the local oral history seems to come from the fact that most Islanders recount their stories to fellow Islanders who serve as a corrective influence. It is not that oral history is "recited" but that information is continually exchanged.

I found that when I interviewed two or more Islanders together, each participant would not allow the others to pass along information they felt was incorrect. Comments like "Oh no, he's not the one who owned that cat boat, that was so-and-so," or "She wasn't the daughter of Henry L., that was her uncle. Her father was Henry M., the one who lived over on the South Road" were frequent. The speaker might then object to this correction or clarification, going carefully through several generations to clarify a genealogical relationship. Or the informants would review an entire incident step by step, mulling each detail and discussing each nuance.

One informant jokingly referred to this as "a lot of bickering between old men," but in fact, something important was occurring. Major and minor details, trivial facts, and incidental happenings all have their place in local history. Convincing a fellow Islander that one's version of a story was the true or correct one required facts. Usually, if two people's versions of a story differed, after a long and detailed discussion one would usually concede that the other was right, not out of politeness but because sufficient proof had been furnished to change his or her mind. Usually the name or date or story under consideration was tied in with several threads of information that the person was already familiar with. "You remember Asa? Well, he was Asa's uncle, and he's the one with the dairy farm up on the hill who owned that beautiful old schooner. And his daughter married Allen Brewer who was your cousin." Because it was such a small island, the discussants could draw on a number of different memories to substantiate a fact. It was rare that only one line of argument was offered to shore up the point.

Of course, in many cases the two people would stick to their own versions of a story, often because of family ties and personal loyalties. One nineteenth-century whaling captain was referred to as "a fine, upstanding, god-fearing man," by his granddaughters, who added, "No one was better loved in this part of the Island." Several weeks later the daughter of a crew member of the captain, who had severely flogged that sailor during a voyage to China, called the captain "little short of a skunk." Similarly, one man, recalling an old-timer, admitted that he might have been a bit feebleminded, but his sister objected vigorously. She'd always thought the man was rather intelligent, "just a bit off, you know." Obviously, any research based on oral history must take into account the many factors that affect the answers given.

Oral history is more than simply a way to confirm information from written sources. Many things never enter written accounts—the mundane facets of every-day life, neighborhood events and characters, gossip, scandal, and misconduct. Quite often it is only through oral history that one can get full knowledge of an individual or incident, even if it is mentioned in a written record. And in a good number of cases in this study, the written records turned out to be wrong, and the oral information much more accurate.

. . . .

Perceived Causes of Vineyard Deafness

People have speculated about the causes of deafness for centuries, but in the latter half of the nineteenth century, doctors and scientists took a renewed interest in deafness, much as polio became a focus in the 1940s and 1950s, and cancer is today. The reasons for this upsurge in interest are not entirely clear. The deaf population had not increased, although the first censuses and the growing number of schools for the deaf made it apparent that there were many more deaf Americans than had previously been estimated. Also, scientists were seeking a single explanation for deafness, and the intense interest in the subject eventually subsided, as scholars realized there was no one basic key to this multifaceted problem. To understand why Vineyarders were confused about the cause of deafness, one must survey the more prominent nineteenth-century theories on the causes of deafness.

• Maternal Fright

Many Vineyarders, along with some leading medical authorities of the time, believed that deafness, like many other congenital disorders, was the direct result of maternal fright—sometimes called marking or maternal anxiety—the effect on the unborn infant of psychological stress on the mother (see Seiss 1887).

In the first volume of *American Annals of the Deaf and Dumb*[1] in 1847, a report provided evidence of the effects of maternal fright on the fetus. Interestingly, although the location was identified as "a small town in the southeastern part of Massachusetts," the exact correlation of names, dates, and numbers of children makes clear that it was certainly Chilmark. The author was uncertain of the validity of maternal fright as the cause of deafness but felt it should be discussed. He stated, incorrectly, that none of the mothers had ever seen a deaf individual before, which made a stronger case for marking. In fact, not only were all these women from either Chilmark or West Tisbury, they were all closely related to one or more persons who were born deaf. The deafness described closely followed a recessive pattern of inheritance, but the author, unaware of the laws of heredity, was seeking to make a different point and completely missed the clues modern scientists would pick out. He wrote:

> Mrs. M., the mother of the four oldest of these mutes, at the time a widow, gave the following account. "A few months previous to the birth of my second child, I went to the funeral of a neighbor. While at the grave, the singular appearance of a young woman attracted my attention. Someone standing near me told me she was deaf and dumb. As I had never seen a person in her condition before, I watched her movements with great interest. As the coffin was lowered into the grave she clasped her hands, raised her eyes and with a peculiar expression of grief and surprise, uttered such a cry as I had never in my life heard before. Her image was before me by day and night for weeks, and her unnatural voice was constantly ringing in my ears. In due time my child was born, and as I feared, proved to be deaf and dumb. In early life, whenever surprised into a sudden exclamation, the sound of his voice was the same as hers. Of my nine children, four were visited with this calamity."
>
> The nearest neighbor of this family was Mr. S. Soon after his marriage he brought his wife home, where she saw the children of Mrs. M., the first deaf and dumb persons she had ever seen. The impression made upon her mind by the misfortune of her neighbor was similar to what had already been described, and with similar results. Her first child was born deaf and dumb as was also her fourth child. The third family in which there were mutes, was that of Capt. T. His wife, previous to her marriage, had never seen a deaf and dumb person. Soon after coming to

her new home, she was introduced to her neighbors, Mrs. M. and S., where she saw their children and was much affected by their unfortunate condition. A knowledge of the supposed cause of their deafness and the apprehension that it might have the same effect in her case, added much to her concern. Her first child was born deaf and dumb, and also her third and fourth. The other neighbor, Mr. L., who had two deaf children, gave a very similar account of the matter in regard to his wife, ascribing the deafness of his children to the same cause. (Turner 1847:28–29)

Examples of maternal fright crowded the nineteenth-century scientific literature. Hawkins felt sure enough of this effect to state that "nine out of every ten mothers of congenitally deaf children attribute their being so to powerfully operating causes upon the mind during gestation" (1863:17). He made the same mistake as Turner had twenty years earlier, confusing marking and heredity. "It also not unfrequently happens that the birth of one deaf child is followed by others similarly afflicted, as if the defect of the former one had so wrought upon the mother's nervous susceptibility as to cause, in subsequent births, that very result, which she so naturally dreaded and wished to avoid."

Even though some doubted that such experiences directly affected the child in utero, the data seemed too strong to dismiss the possibility. Gallaudet, addressing the Royal Commission in London in 1888, explained:

In cases of congenital deafness, maternal anxiety, to which many cases are ascribed, with what degree of truth it would be presumptuous now to judge, may sometimes become epidemic. At least there are certain years in which the nervous system of females is rendered more than usually excitable, and shocks that may have a deleterious influence on the offspring are more common. This is particularly the case in a country that is the seat of war. Many mothers in France have ascribed the infirmity of their congenitally deaf children to alarms sustained during the invasion of France by the Allies in 1814 and 1815, and its subsequent occupation. (Gallaudet 1892:45)

Alexander Graham Bell, though he disagreed strongly with the explanation of maternal fright, said that "in my examination and inquiries among parents I found that belief very prevalent" (1892:11).

• Environment

Some Vineyarders, along with many nineteenth-century scientists, believed that climate or geography might be the ultimate cause of deafness. One local author even suggested that the salty air on the south side of the Island caused the deafness.

Even Bell, at his wits' end trying to explain the deafness on the Vineyard, considered environment as a cause when he addressed the Royal Commission of the United Kingdom in 1886:

> The appearance of deafness is confined to that particular part of the island. The geological character of that part of the island is different from the rest of the island. The surface is undulating and hilly whereas the rest of the island is flat. It has a subsoil of very curious variegated clays that crop out in the form of a bold headland that is so beautifully colored by these clays to have acquired the name of Gay Head. Whether that has anything to do with the deafness I do not know, but it is a very curious fact that it is that part of the island alone where the deafness occurs although the bulk of the population lies outside. (Bell 1892:53)

Bell apparently did not consider the fact that deafness was unknown among the Gay Head Indians, who mined the clay deposits for the local paint mill.

For centuries writers had tried to draw some correlation between deafness and the environment. Bulwer, in the first book published in English on deafness, drew from many classical Greek and Roman writers. In accounting for forms of deafness caused by factors other than readily apparent disease, he wrote: "The causes [for deafness] are various and unknowne. There are those who suppose that this happens to some through the propriety of their place of birth. Soranus affirmes that those who are borne in Ships at Sea, are by proprietie of their place of birth, like Fishes, mute" (1648:76–77). Bulwer, like many other writers, confused heredity with environment when he wrote: "Munto confidently affirmes, that by a proprietie of place, they who were borne within the walls of the castle of Claramont, proved dumbe; as it happened to all the Barons that were borne there." Taking as fact the folktale that those who lived near the "Caturrachs of the Nile" were all deafened by the thunderous noise, Bulwer speculated as to whether this population "are not commonly borne deafe also, rather than afterwards so made" (79–80).

• Will of God

Both in Europe and America deafness, as well as many birth defects and diseases, was often attributed to the will of God, generally as a warning or punishment. This folk belief appeared in Biblical accounts and throughout Western literature (Hand 1980:67). Bulwer, in 1648, provided an example. "Sometimes the sinnes of the Parents are exemplarily punished in their children," he wrote. One deaf child's inability to hear was directly attributed to its mother's conduct: "He is an example of God's justice for, his mother being accused of stealing when shee went with Childe with him, used such an imprecation, that if that which she was charged with was true, her Childe might never speake when it came to be in the World, but remaine Dumbe all his life" (1648:77–78).

This belief in divine retribution was found among the early Puritan settlers in New England, although we do not know how common it was. Governor Winthrop reported a "monsterous birth"—a child born with two mouths, no forehead, and claws (probably anencephalic with an open myelomeningocele). Though the child's parents were considered upright citizens, Winthrop could clearly perceive God's wrath in the incident, as both of them were followers of the heretical Mrs. Hutchinson. Increase Mather, in a book written in 1684, cited several cases of disabilities in children as the result of God's displeasure, and Cotton Mather, his son, noted further examples in his history of Puritan Massachusetts.

Throughout the seventeenth, eighteenth, and nineteenth centuries, the occurrence of deafness and other disabilities was commonly viewed as a judgment by God. In a letter published in the *American Annals of the Deaf* a deaf gentleman from Iowa stated: "It is part of the punishment inflicted for violation of nature's laws, which violation—whether it comes from carelessness, design or ignorance—results in deafness, blindness, lameness, etc., and will so result until man has so far improved, mentally, morally and physically, that diseases and accidents of a severe nature will be unknown" (Booth 1858, 1:77).

Such explanations were common (Jacobs 1869:21). In 1847 a Mr.

T., father of four deaf children, stated that "he regarded it as a judge-
ment from Heaven for having married his cousin" (Turner 1847:30).
And Carlin, speculating on the ultimate cause of deafness, wrote:

> The generality of this unfortunate class of beings enjoy the ben-
> efits of all the senses except that of hearing, of which they are
> deprived by the wise Providence, for their good. (Query: if a deaf-
> mute child is born of deaf-mute parents, to which is its apparent
> misfortune to be attributed, to its parents, as some affirm, or to
> God's own pleasure and judgement for its future good?) (Carlin
> 1851:53)

Brooks offered what was probably the best compromise between the
concepts of God's will and heredity, arguing that "if by an adequate
census it shall appear that the five thousand couples who married first-
cousins have from three hundred and fifty to four hundred imbecile
or peculiar children, then it will be proved that the marriage of first-
cousins is forbidden of God" (Brooks 1855:238).

Whether divine retribution was ever considered a cause of deafness
on the Vineyard is not known. None of my informants ever offered it
as an explanation. Only a handful of the informants had ever heard
this explanation, and those who had, had heard it from off-Islanders.
They rejected this idea out of hand. If the folk belief in divine retribution came to the Island with the early Puritan settlers, it seems to
have long since disappeared.

• Other Theories

One of the older deaf Islanders told a reporter from the *Boston Sunday
Herald* in 1895 that he thought deafness was "catching, just like
diphtheria and small pox." A Mr. Sanborn, secretary to the Board of
Health, Lunacy and Charity for the state of Massachusetts, in a letter
to Bell in 1884, wrote that the prevalence of deafness on Martha's
Vineyard "was due to special causes irrespective of descent from a
common ancestor." As evidence, Sanborn cited the case of a deaf
Vineyard couple who, though distantly related, attributed the deafness
of several of their children to the fact that "the husband was twenty
years older than his wife" (Sanborn 1884).

A traditional rivalry between two of the largest up-Island families was often jokingly invoked when the subject of deafness came up. Both families had had large numbers of deaf individuals, and as one man told me: "The Norths were always saying they'd of been all right if they hadn't of married the Brewers, and the Brewers were always saying as how they'd of been fine if they had not married into the Norths."

Perhaps the simplest explanation was offered by a man from West Tisbury, who attributed the Island deafness to vanity. "It was the women's fault, you know," he explained. When I looked somewhat puzzled, he continued, "They would wear their corset stays too tight, and it'd damage the babies." Such explanations were not uncommon (Newman 1969), and the man adamantly stuck to his beliefs through the long discussion of genetics that followed.

Notes

1. "They Were Just Like Everyone Else"

1. Native Islanders divided the world into two parts—the Island and off-Island. Off-Island refers to the mainland (sometimes called the continent). Going off-Island may mean going to New Bedford for the day or to China for ten years. Vineyarders also make a distinction between down-Island—the eastern part, including the towns of Edgartown, Oak Bluffs, and Tisbury—and up-Island to the west, including West Tisbury, Chilmark, and Gay Head. These names are derived from nautical terms. To sail eastward is to run a vessel "down" its longitude toward the prime meridian in Greenwich. To sail westward is to run "up" the longitude. Using this same system Islanders spoke of going up to New York and down to Maine (Huntington 1969:15).

2. Islanders traditionally referred to deaf individuals as being deaf and dumb, or occasionally as deaf-mutes. Both terms are inaccurate and outdated. In the mid-nineteenth century the old English term "deaf and dumb" was gradually replaced in America by the term "deaf-mute" (Gordon 1892). These terms imply that those who cannot hear are also unable to make sounds. However, except in extremely rare instances, a deaf person's lack of speech is solely the result of his inability to hear and reproduce the sounds. Almost all deaf people are capable of producing sounds, and certainly all those on Martha's Vineyard were. Both "deaf-mute" and "deaf and dumb" have acquired pejorative connotations and in recent years have been replaced by the term deaf (Fraser 1964). But in Martha's Vineyard the terms are not pejorative, and I have retained them in all quotes.

3. Among the known instances of recessive deafness in small, inbred communities are: a Scottish clan, Jewish communities in Britain (Fraser 1976);

Little Cayman Island (Doran 1952); the Swiss commune of Ayent (Secretan 1954; Hanhart 1962); the Dutch village of Katwijk (Aulbers 1959); the Amish and Mennonites of Lancaster County, Pennsylvania (Mengel et al. 1967; McKusick 1978); the village of Adamarobe, Ghana (David et al. 1971); a clan of Jicaque Indians in Honduras (Chapman and Jacquard 1971); the Guntar area of Andhra Pradesh, India (Majumdar 1972); the Mayan Indian village of Nohya (Shuman 1980a, 1980b); Providence Island in the Caribbean (Washabaugh, Woodward, and DeSantis 1978; Washabaugh 1980a, b); and ethnic enclaves in Israel (Costeff and Dar 1980).

4. The earliest attempt to enumerate the number of deaf persons in the United States was an article by Francis Green in the *New England Palladium* in October 1803 (Green 1861; Bell 1899); the first effective, organized effort was through the 1830 federal census. Estimates of the number of deaf persons in the country varied drastically from one decade to the next, reflecting changes in demography, epidemiology, and census-taking practices. All of the nineteenth-century federal censuses were disputed by at least one, and usually more, of the experts on deafness (*American Annals of the Deaf* 1848; 1852; 1873; 1874b; H. Peet 1852; Seiss 1887; Bell 1892; Gallaudet 1892; United States Department of Commerce 1918). *Harper's New Monthly Magazine* (1874) found that the data on deafness in the 1870 federal census was "inconsistent with itself."

Most of the censuses have so many inaccuracies that they provide only the vaguest idea of the actual number of deaf people in the country. The figure given in the text is an attempt to estimate prevalence based on those figures of the number of deaf people listed in the federal censuses from 1830 to 1900. Although statistics do not exist for earlier centuries, there is no reason to believe that they would be significantly different from those for the nineteenth century.

5. Goffman argued that those who are in some way deviant from the norm can be considered to have a social stigma, something that is felt to be "deeply discrediting . . . a failing, a shortcoming, a handicap" (Goffman 1963:3). Their identity is said to be spoiled. To use Mary Douglas's (1966) theoretical construct, they are "polluted" or "impure." Edgerton (1976) has cautioned that while all societies recognize deviance, what is considered deviant may vary from culture to culture. However, it has been a virtually unquestioned assumption that all types of handicapped individuals can be grouped together and that by definition they are all seen by the larger society as deviant. The best that the handicapped man or woman can do, we are told, is to pretend to be normal by ignoring those physical or mental attributes that are usually glaringly apparent to all "normal" people. Davis (1964) termed this stance "deviance disavowal," a concept that merely strengthens the idea of deviance

by assuming there is a norm against which people can measure themselves to confirm or deny their own worth.

The specific categorization of disabilities as deviance is the *social* response to a mental or physical attribute. As Goffman succinctly stated, "Society establishes the means of categorizing persons and the complement of attributes felt to be ordinary and natural for members of each of these categories" (1963:2). These concepts offer significant insights into many of the problems disabled people face in our society, not because they necessarily reflect a disabled individual's concept of self-worth, but because they help to explain the social milieu in which he or she must act and react.

6. Many authors, assuming that handicaps are seen in the same way in all cultures, fail to offer a satisfactory definition of what they consider to be a handicap or disability. It is important that the terminology be precise. There are a number of different definitions of what constitutes an impairment, a disability, or a handicap. The terms used vary from author to author and from discipline to discipline, often being only a question of semantics. According to the World Health Organization (WHO), between 3 and 10 percent of the world's population suffer some sort of disability that is congenital or caused by disease or accident. WHO (Wood 1980) presents a sequence, as shown in the figure below, of illness-related phenomena (including birth defects) that makes some useful distinctions.

An impairment is "any loss of or abnormality of psychological, physiological, or anatomical structure or function." A disability reflects the consequences of an impairment, being any restriction or lack of ability to perform an activity in the manner or within the range considered normal for nonimpaired persons. A handicap, a disadvantage resulting from an impairment or disability, limits or prevents the person from fulfilling his or her normal role. Handicaps therefore are not determined by one's physical capabilities but rather reflect the social consequences of that disability. In short, the individual's perception of a handicap is tempered by the society in which the person lives.

7. Only two deaf men were considered to be handicapped, according to the Islanders. The first, a farmer and fisherman, had lost his right hand in a mowing machine accident as a teenager, and hence was said to be handicapped. He used a special leather strap to help him work and row, and he was

able to maintain his family well. Indeed, he was considered the best duck shot and one of the best boatmen in town—no mean feat on an island of expert boatmen. The other handicapped deaf individual apparently had difficulty walking. A big, impressively strong fisherman, he had stepped on a scythe blade and cut all the tendons on the bottom of his foot. He limped very badly for the rest of his life.

8. Beginning in 1830 in both national and state censuses, a column was reserved for the census taker to indicate whether the person listed was deaf, blind, insane, or "idiotic." These were the only regular records of deafness. Unfortunately, their reliability was continually questioned throughout the nineteenth century. Leading experts on deafness argued that the deaf listed were severely underrepresented because families were reluctant to provide census takers with "embarrassing" aspects of their family history. This may have been a problem in larger cities, where census takers did not know each family, but it is probably not valid for the Vineyard, where the census takers were neighbors who knew everyone in the family, and no embarrassment was involved.

In the 1830 and 1840 censuses the deaf were not listed by name unless they were the heads of households. Instead, the census would report a family of six with "one deaf-mute under 16 years of age" or "two deaf-mute adolescents in household of parents"—hardly an accurate picture of a household with nine or ten children below the age of fourteen. In 1850 deaf individuals began to be listed by name.

Even later, when censuses accurately recorded the names and ages of all deaf individuals, there were still difficulties. A national or state census was taken every five years, but it is quite conceivable that in that interval a young deaf child might die or the family might move off-Island. Or a baby's deafness may not have been recognized at the first census. Hence if a child was born in 1840 and died in 1844, no mention of his deafness might be preserved. Oral history is particularly weak concerning very young children, and the death of a young deaf child might go unmentioned. We cannot assume that the number of children who died were an insignificant proportion of the population. In the United States in the nineteenth century, a child had a one-in-four chance of dying before the age of five (J. Bell 1859). At least a quarter of all Island children apparently died before the age of twenty-one (Banks 1966:3).

There is another reason to suspect that during the seventeenth, eighteenth, and early nineteenth centuries the rate of deafness was higher than the records indicate. About the year 1835, when current oral history begins, the rate of known deafness increased dramatically. Quite possibly the earlier incidence of deafness on the Island was higher than can now be ascertained.

9. Eighty percent of my primary informants were between the ages of seventy-five and ninety. Seven were over ninety, and the oldest was ninety-seven. Because most of the Island's deaf inhabitants had died before 1920, people in their sixties knew far less about them, although I did obtain information from a woman in her middle forties, who had, as a child, known one of the last of the deaf Island women as a babysitter.

10. For the formal interview sessions, I used a tape recorder; for shorter sessions, I took notes. I told all my informants why I was collecting information and what I planned to use it for. At no time was the tape recorder turned on without my informant's full knowledge and express consent, and all informants were told they could ask to have the tape turned off or erased at any point during or after the interview. (Fortunately, no one ever asked me to erase a tape, and only one or two asked me to turn the tape recorder off when the story was considered too trivial for me to "waste my tape" on.) When a quote is given in the text, it is included because at least two, and often more, informants told me similar stories, or because the story was consistent with all other information I had on that person or incident. Because much of the material is personal or subjective, I have not identified the individuals quoted.

11. For example, dozens of stories are still told about the great days of whaling and about those who were part of the whaling industry, including numerous stories about the year the entire Arctic whaling fleet was crushed in the ice off Alaska. In many cases each family has different stories about the same event. In contrast, I was able to collect only a handful of stories about the Revolutionary War, and most were very similar to the accounts in Banks's *History of Martha's Vineyard*. My informants were aware of this. "Look it up in Banks," I was frequently told by someone seeking to verify an ancestor's role in the Revolution. "He makes mention of it." Banks's material was culled largely from the Island's oral history over the course of several decades, but once set in print, it seems to have become the standard reference.

12. Richard Pease, the first real Island historian, was by the 1880s an elderly man who had assembled a lifetime of research on Vineyard history. He hoped to write the definitive work on Martha's Vineyard, but apparently he was never able to pull his vast collection of notes together for anything more than an occasional article on Island genealogy for a local newspaper (Banks 1966).

In return for the use of Pease's material, Bell offered to pay for the publication of Pease's Island history, but the elderly Pease did not live long enough to put the manuscript into any sort of intelligible form. In a kind gesture, Bell wrote to Pease's widow, who was in straitened circumstances, and offered to pay her an amount of money comparable to what it would have cost to publish the Island history (Bell 1913). If she would rather, Bell mentioned, he could give her instead $2,500 in stock from his newly founded company, Bell Telephone. With true Yankee caution, Mrs. Pease replied to Bell's letter by saying she could not trust her financial security to some new invention with an uncertain future. She took the cash. Whether she ever realized that $2,500 in original Bell Telephone Company stock would have made her an extremely wealthy woman is not known. (Bell notes, Hitz Memorial Library; Library of Congress, private correspondence.)

13. Bell did much of the research himself. He had two assistants, Annie F. Pratt of Chelsea, Massachusetts, a professional genealogist, and Harriet Marshall Pease, daughter of Richard Pease, who was exceptionally knowledgeable about the Island. Bell collected data over a four-year period.

14. According to a letter written by Bell to Fred Deland some thirty years later (Bell 1913), one copy of the notes was lost when the house of Mrs. Pratt, Bell's assistant, burned to the ground. Another copy, reported in a newspaper article to have been deposited at the Massachusetts Historical Society (*Boston Sunday Herald* 1895), does not appear to have actually been placed there.

15. Bell, in his letter to Deland, recalled that the master copy of his research had been placed in "large flat draws" in the "Volta Bureau" (an organization founded by Bell, which would later bear his own name).

Unfortunately, the Hitz Memorial Library had no record of having these notes. Some time later I stopped at the Hitz Memorial Library to see if they could suggest where the Bell manuscripts may have been deposited. Salome Swaim, a new librarian there, was in the midst of reorganizing and cataloguing their extensive collections. Less than a week before, she had found, in storage in a warehouse in Virginia, two large cardboard boxes containing all of Bell's missing notes on Martha's Vineyard deafness.

Dr. Sarah Conlon, the director of the Alexander Graham Bell Association, was kind enough to have the notes brought out of storage immediately so I could begin to go through them—and therefore it is to Ms. Swaim, Dr. Conlon, and the other members of the staff at the Alexander Graham Bell Foundation that I owe a major debt of gratitude, both for retrieving the notes and for being so pleasant and helpful during the week I spent at their facility looking through these boxes.

16. Bell went to Chilmark to collect genealogies and spent at least one "prolonged visit there" (*Vineyard Gazette* 1922). He must have heard stories about what life was like for the early deaf Islanders, but he did not record any. Nor did he mention in his correspondence anything about what we know to have been the then-active use of sign language by both hearing and deaf people on the Vineyard.

Bell was certainly aware of the social and linguistic implications of deafness in the community, because several years later he directed a colleague's attention to this wide use of sign language. The colleague, whose name is unknown, went to the Vineyard to meet these deaf people in the mid-1890s and wrote a short article on them for the *Boston Sunday Herald,* which was reprinted widely in papers throughout the country.

At the time of Bell's research on the Vineyard, he was one of the nation's foremost advocates of teaching the deaf to lip read rather than use sign language. He initially became involved with the deaf community through teaching lip reading, and the purpose of his research on hereditary deafness was to substantiate his theory that without the formal knowledge of speaking, the deaf would tend to congregate together because of their common sign language, marry one another, and finally produce a "deaf variety of the human race" (Bell 1883).

The Vineyard, with its easy bilingual community and free intermarriage of the deaf and the hearing, must have seemed to Bell completely inexplicable. For Bell to have published a study taking into account the social aspects of Vineyard deafness would have contradicted many of his most cherished beliefs. This is not to say that Bell was intellectually dishonest—indeed, he appears to have been exacting in his research. But he seems to have viewed the social situation on the Vineyard as an anomaly. Ignoring his experience on the Vineyard altogether, he stated to the Royal Commission in England ten years later that "the sign language is not of any value whatever in promoting social intercourse with the hearing; its value as a means of social intercourse is with deaf-mutes alone. It promotes their intercourse with one another, but hearing people do not know it" (Bell 1892:64).

2. *The History of Martha's Vineyard*

1. Geographically and historically, two other islands have always been associated with Martha's Vineyard and will be considered as part of the Vineyard here. Across a channel off the extreme eastern end of the Island lies the small island of Chappaquiddick, and two and a half miles south of the Vineyard lies the still smaller island of Nomans Land.

2. Although the Elizabeth Islands are seven miles away, across Vineyard Sound and immediately adjacent to the mainland, the chain was included in the original purchase agreement and still remains part of Dukes County. However, they have always been far more closely linked with the nearby areas of Cape Cod and southeastern Massachusetts. Several Vineyard surnames appear with some frequency on the Elizabeths, because the lineages go back to the same early families from the Barnstable-Sandwich-Falmouth area. Recessive deafness did not exist in the Elizabeth Islands and hence I do not discuss them here.

3. Ritchie (1969:3) estimated the Indian population at the time of contact

as 1,500 to 1,600, but he did not indicate what data those figures were based on. The Island historian Charles Banks estimated the population in prehistorical times as near 3,000 (1966, vol. 1). Gale Huntington (personal communication), who is writing a history of the Indians on Martha's Vineyard, believes the population may have been even higher. White diseases took a heavy toll on the native Indian population, and their numbers dropped precipitously. Pushed to the far western edge of the Island, these Indians managed to maintain much of their own cultural heritage, and their population eventually began to grow again.

4. The source of the Island's name remains a mystery, although Huntington (1969) considers the explanation that links the name with Gosnold to be the best, and it is the most common one in the local oral tradition (Banks 1966, vol. 1). Banks does mention that "in the public and private records of the 17th century, the name of 'Martin's' is applied to the Vineyard to the practical exclusion of 'Martha's' " (Banks 1966, 1:73). In either case the profusion of grapevines on the Island earned it the name "Vineyard." The similarity of this name to the Vikings' Vineland has prompted some Island historians to suggest that the Vineyard is the actual Viking site. There is absolutely no evidence to support that claim.

5. Undated entry in Winthrop's *Journal*, between December 3, 1643, and January 18, 1644. Before 1752, dates between January 1 and March 25 were double-dated: 1634/5, 1711/2. I have changed all such dates to the later year: 1711/2 = 1712.

6. To give an idea of the amount of traffic, David F. Chase, skipper of the Pigs and Sows lightship at the western entrance of the Sound reported that in 1845 alone, 13,814 vessels had been sighted during daylight hours. Some of those vessels may have been sighted repeatedly, but the number of those that passed unseen at night probably balances the repetition to some degree (Huntington 1969).

3. The Origins of Vineyard Deafness

1. Medical records might have been of some assistance in defining the extent and nature of Vineyard deafness, but none seem to have survived. The first physician on the Island did not arrive until the last quarter of the seventeenth century, and doctors with formal training were rare for a long time after that (Banks 1966, vol. 1). Although major illnesses such as smallpox, consumption, and throat distemper (diphtheria) were mentioned in local accounts, assessment of medical problems was often sketchy even when there were physicians. I found no report of any clinical examination of the middle ear or external ear canals of a deaf Islander; probably no records were ever written. There are no reports that the hearing of an individual born deaf ever

improved, and no deaf person attempted to gain hearing through any medical procedure. A number of these deaf people lived well into the twentieth century. If they had thought that their hearing could have been restored, one would suppose that some would at least have discussed such a step with their relatives. No surviving relatives recall any discussion of this sort.

2. This is not to say that no cases of deafness on the Vineyard resulted from accident or illness. Given the statistics for the Vineyard population, which averaged 3,100 individuals throughout the first three centuries of settlement, one would expect two cases of deafness from disease, accident, or old age to regularly be present in the population. In fact, from the early nineteenth century, when records begin, through to the present several Islanders did lose their hearing through accident or illness, an incidence which is consistent with national statistics on acquired deafness.

Individuals with partial hearing loss or deafness caused by disease or old age are readily identified through both oral history and census returns. Islanders made a distinction between those born deaf (deaf and dumb) and those who were simply deaf or very hard of hearing. In the latter case they often explained how the hearing loss had occurred. Moreover, census reports correlated with this oral history in all cases: individuals initially not listed as deaf are subsequently listed as such, usually in later life. In one instance, a young child, who was initially listed as hearing, was later listed as deaf within a year of the time his family recalled an accident had led to his hearing loss. In no case were any of the Vineyarders who had been born deaf listed as hearing. None of those Vineyarders who had acquired forms of deafness have been included in this study.

Four deaf individuals (one older man, a young adult, and two children, both from off-Island families), currently live on the Island, but their deafness is apparently not the old Island hereditary form, so they have not been included.

3. In only one case did an Island deaf woman who was married to an off-Island deaf man with no Vineyard ancestors have a deaf child. However, the off-Island man's family (the Browns of Henniker, New Hampshire) had a dominant form of hereditary deafness. In three generations, thirty-four deaf individuals were born in this family (Cogswell 1880). The deaf offspring of this marriage are not included in the statistics on Vineyard deafness.

4. Geneticists disagree about how many mutant alleles for severe recessive deafness exist in the human population (Chung, Robinson, and Morton 1959; Morton 1960; Sank 1963; Fraser 1964; Chung and Brown 1970; Fraser 1976; Costeff and Dar 1980). As McKusick (1978) noted, the number of recessive genes for deafness (and other disorders) may be considerably higher than is currently thought; small families and outbreeding result in their not being expressed in most populations.

5. For example, one of the sons of the first Tilton in New England moved

to New Jersey in the mid-seventeenth century, at about the same time his brother moved to Martha's Vineyard. Three generations later, two descendants of Tilton in New Jersey married each other (they would have been third cousins once removed). He was the only ancestor they had in common. Two offspring of this marriage were born deaf, the first to appear in this New Jersey line. Their deafness appears to have been identical to that found on Martha's Vineyard among their long-lost relatives. Hence, it must be assumed that Robert Tilton and/or his wife, were carriers of the gene. The pedigree (taken from Bell's notes, John Hitz Memorial Library) looks as follows:

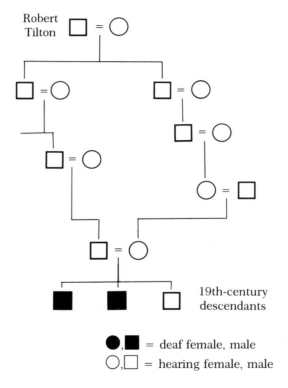

19th-century descendants

●,■ = deaf female, male
○,□ = hearing female, male

6. Intermarriage among the local gentry was particularly common in Kent (Everitt 1966), where more than two-thirds of the minor gentry married people from adjoining towns. In the Weald this figure was even higher. There, noted Everitt, "All the gentry came of original Kentish stock." The further one went

south from London into the Weald, the more marked this became. Around Maidstone, over half of the gentry married others from Kent, and in Ashford, this figure rose to 85 percent. Chalkins (1965), writing of the Weald in the seventeenth century, added that there was "constant intermarriage" among these people. Indeed, "so inbred were the gentry that when Mary Honeywood died in the 1630's, her 367 descendants had brought nearly all the gentry of Kent into a single genealogical tree" (Everitt 1956:8). Laslett, speaking of seventeenth-century Kentish gentry specifically, wrote: "The country community was held together by blood as well as class. The genealogical interrelationships between its members were extensive, complicated and meticulously observed by all of them; it is astonishing how distant a connection qualified for the title 'cozen' " (1948:150).

7. Hagaman, Elias, and Netting (1978), in a study of a Swiss alpine village, found that an endogamous population was not necessarily a genetic isolate. In that community in-migrants had more descendants than locals, and hence for many generations had a significant impact on the diversity of the gene pool. However, Hagaman and her associates did not take into consideration the fact that the in-migrants came predominantly from villages in the immediately surrounding area with long histories of marriage into the village under study. If endogamy and inbreeding are viewed in a neighborhood pattern, I suspect that more neighborhoods might be considered genetic isolates. Hagaman's point, then, is important. Geographical boundaries should not lead us to assume that endogamy or inbreeding exists, but also they should not interfere with conceptualizing genetics in regional terms.

8. I am indebted to Peter Dunkley, senior producer for the British Broadcasting Corporation's series on sign language, for this reference, and the information on Downing. Mr. Dunkley was kind enough to arrange research time for me at the County archives in Maidstone, and he helped me look through some of the materials for references to deafness.

9. During the 1630s, New England was still very much a wilderness. Travel was extremely difficult and often dangerous. Early settlers of Cape Cod and the Vineyard rarely ventured far from home, and when business or legal affairs necessitated some travel, the destination was usually Plymouth, center of Plymouth Colony, rather than Boston.

10. By the end of the 1630s, there were well-established nonconformist congregations in the Weald towns of Ashford, Benenden, Bethersden, Biddenden, Cranbrook, Egerton, Maidstone, Marden, Staplehurst, and Tenterden, the northern edges of the Weald and central Kent (Chalkins 1965).

11. Lothrop, an Oxford-educated minister, had originally been ordained in the Church of England and had been settled in the parish of Egerton in the Weald in 1611 (Neal 1754). This congregation had a long radical tradition

and at the time of Lothrop's arrival "was probably one of the leading separatist congregations" (Clark 1977:327). Lothrop became an ardent separatist and attracted a large and loyal following. In 1623 he went to London, where he was chosen as pastor of a Congregational church in Southwark (Deyo 1890). For six or seven years Lothrop clandestinely preached to his London congregation of perhaps sixty followers (Neal 1754), evidently still maintaining close ties to his former congregation in the Weald. In the spring of 1632 he was arrested "for witnessing against the errours of the times" (257). Packed off to jail, Lothrop steadfastly refused to refute his religious beliefs.

In 1634 he was granted his freedom on condition he leave the country immediately (Pratt 1929). This he did. With him went a number of his flock, including some members of his London congregation (Deane 1831). But the core of the group seems to have been members of his Kentish congregation. As Banks stated: "Reverend John Lothrop, who had been vicar of Egerton, Kent . . . was undoubtedly the inspiration for the emigration of a large contingent from the Weald of Kent" (1930:19).

12. In fact, the term "men of Kent" is an even more specific designation than it seems. In Kent it was applied only to those people from the eastern part of the county. Those from the western part were called "Kentish men" (Clark 1977). Jerrold (1907) referred to the distinction as "a commonly accepted difference," and defined "men of Kent" as those born east and south of the river Medway, while Kentish men were those born to the west of that river. The Weald lies east and south of the Medway, the heart of the district from which "men of Kent" come.

13. There is good evidence to support a similar number of wives, children, and servants for the remaining twenty men. Of the immigrants who came during this period, Banks wrote: "As a rule, these emigrants were people in early middle life, generally married with a few young children . . . Very few aged people undertook the dangerous ocean voyage unless accompanying their married sons or daughters" (1963:xv). Although documentation is lacking, each of these twenty men is listed, within five years of their arrival in Massachusetts, as married with several children.

14. A number of problems crop up when one attempts to establish the English origins of many early New England settlers. England had no civil registration of births, deaths, or marriages until 1837. Although the church established a system of registration for baptisms, marriages, and deaths as early as 1538, the local clergy were often lax in maintaining parish records, and many records have also been lost or destroyed over the years. Hence, although it is occasionally possible to trace the genealogy of individuals of yeoman stock back to 1538, a complete record is quite rare (Banks 1963). Only the wealthier people made wills. Dudley (1973) estimated that between

a third and a half of all townsmen in Kent lived near the subsistence level, and few of them would have made wills.

There is an additional problem concerning marriage and baptismal records. As Banks summarized it: "Marriages took place, in the large majority of cases, at the bride's home, and unless residence of the groom was specifically stated, he may have come from a distant parish. Also, it was the custom of the period to baptize the eldest child in the former home of the mother" (1963:xxi). All these factors complicated the process of locating the home parishes of the early settlers.

On passenger lists of vessels going to America, usually only the individual's most recent home in England was given. A number of those from the Weald were tradesmen who moved to larger towns or cities to apprentice and follow their trade. Though listed as being "from Sandwich" or "from London," a more thorough study of the records shows that these were men from Kent, joining their old townsmen in relocating to the New World. For example, two brothers are recorded as coming from different towns—William Hatch from Ashford in the Weald, his brother from several miles away in Wye. Foxwell, listed as coming from St. Brides, London, was originally from the Weald (Deane 1831).

The two most comprehensive studies of the names and numbers of immigrants are Banks 1930 and 1937. Both are good, as far as they go, but names are frequently omitted, and points of origin in England are sometimes missing or wrong. Far worse, however, is that for the years after 1650 no comprehensive source is available, and documentation on both sides of the Atlantic is much more haphazard for those who did arrive.

15. Damon stated that most of Lothrop's first group was from London, but added, "The same winter, others of their Kentish friends came among them" (1884:407). His basis for stating that most of this group was from London is not known, other than the fact that Lothrop was coming directly from London. All the data I have collected indicates that most of the group was from Kent. It may be that some people who moved from the Weald to London in the early 1600s joined Lothrop's congregation because he had been their family preacher at home. Some of those listed in Lothrop's London congregation undoubtedly had ties to the Weald.

Deyo noted of Lothrop's church that, once at Scituate, "They were joined by thirteen of the church who had previously arrived" (1890:383), and this is substantiated by the church records in Plymouth, which indicated that on November 23, 1634, a number of men were dismissed from the Plymouth congregation "in case they join the body at Scituate" (Freeman 1862, 2:244). Seven of the eight men named as moving from Plymouth to Scituate were from Kent—four from Tenterden, one from Ashford, and the remaining two from unknown Kentish parishes; because of their continuing close associations with individuals from the Weald (Damon 1884), these two were probably also from the Weald.

16. Estimating the population of Scituate in these early years is difficult, as no one list exists. I have assembled the figures in the text from Deane 1831; Pratt 1929; and Banks 1930, 1963. These lists give the names of men only. No adequate information exists for wives, children, and younger male and female servants. Some patterns do begin to emerge, however. I estimate that in 1635 there lived or had lived in Scituate fifty-four men and their families, with fifty-one different surnames (all those with identical surnames being either siblings or fathers and sons). Twenty-six men, nearly half, were "of Kent." For five of these, I was unable to locate their parishes in Kent, but for the other twenty-one, the pattern of immigration from the Weald is striking:

The Weald
    Ashford, 2
    Biddenden, 4
    Egerton, 1
    Hawkhurst, 1
    Tenterden, 8
    Wye, 1
Kent outside the Weald
    Boughton-under-Blean, 1
    East Greenwich, 1
    Sandwich, 1
    Wooton, 1

The distances between the Weald parishes, as can be seen on the map, average about five miles. Eleven of the fifty-four settlers were from parts unknown; some of these may also have been from Kent.

By 1641 ninety-seven men lived or had lived in town, but the regional English origins of this larger group remained about the same. Forty-seven were from Kent, and the concentration of settlers from the Weald is still strikingly high:

The Weald
    Ashford, 2
    Biddenden, 7
    Cranbrook, 1
    Egerton, 1
    Hawkhurst, 2
    Horsmonden, 1
    High Haldon, 1
    Tenterden, 14
    Wye, 2

Kent outside the Weald
  Alkam, 1
  Ash-near-Sandwich, 5
  Boughton-under-Blean, 1
  Canterbury, 1
  Denton, 1
  East Greenwich, 1
  Sandwich, 1
  Wooton, 1
  Parish unknown, 4

Of the remaining fifty, seventeen can be traced to scattered areas of England other than Kent. With the exception of three from Cambridgeshire, those few who came from the same county always were from different townships. "Previous to 1640," wrote Deane, the early historian of Scituate, "most of the population was from the County of Kent in England" (1831:iii).

17. Historians disagree on how many members of the original group in Scituate went to Barnstable. Deyo said it was "the greater part of Mr. Lothrop's church . . . leaving the remaining few in a broken condition" (1890:368); Deane said "nearly half" (1831:iii); and Trayser stated that the move was so popular, it left the Scituate church with only seven male members (1939:9).

18. The heads of twelve of these twenty-five families were undoubtedly from the Kentish Weald, while the English origins of nine more men are in doubt, but some or all may have been from the Weald.

19. By 1640 fifty-three men are believed to have been living within the town limits. One group of new families came from Dorsetshire and Somersetshire by way of the Boston area (Trayser 1939), but many additional people were from Kent, members of the Scituate congregation who could not leave for Barnstable earlier. Some were Kentish men from other New England towns who were just coming to join the still predominantly Kentish community. For several years a few immigrants continued to arrive from Kent to join relatives in the newly founded town of Barnstable.

20. Numbers vary considerably here. A Plymouth census also taken in 1635 listed sixty-one men, twenty-three of whom were from Kent. A list I compiled included seventy-three names, twenty-eight of known Kentish origin. As some of the earliest founders of Barnstable had already moved out of town before 1644, seventy-three is probably far too high a number, reflecting only the *total* in 1644. Whatever the numbers, the percentage of men in Barnstable who were originally from Kent is about 38 percent. Another 30 percent in both censuses are from parts unknown, presumably some also being from Kent. Those from Kent continued to be the largest segment of the population.

21. That the trait for deafness existed in the original group from Kent is

also indicated by the occasional occurrence of "Vineyard deafness" on the mainland, including the first deaf person who settled on the Vineyard. Several cases of hereditary deafness were reported in the lower Cape Cod region in the eighteenth and nineteenth centuries in families with direct ties to the Martha's Vineyard group. Many families that settled in Barnstable, Sandwich, Falmouth, and other Cape Cod towns had come originally from Kent. Although these settlements were never as genetically restricted as the Vineyard, the small population and relatively stable gene pool on Cape Cod meant that some intermarriage did occur. Deafness appeared in at least four families with Kentish ancestry in Barnstable, Sandwich, Falmouth, and Orleans. In each family, several individuals, usually siblings, were deaf. One family on Nantucket had four deaf children; both parents could trace their ancestry directly to Vineyard families and, more remotely, to Lothrop's Kentish contingent. A hearing Vineyard couple that moved to Providence, Rhode Island, had two deaf children, as did a hearing Vineyard couple who moved to California in the late nineteenth century (Groce 1983).

Interestingly, there were no reported cases of deafness in Scituate that appear to be related to the hereditary deafness on Martha's Vineyard. After 1640, when the main contingent of families from Kent left to join Lothrop in Barnstable, Scituate began to attract a much more diversified group of settlers. Lying almost halfway between Boston and Plymouth, it drew new people from both areas (Damon 1885). In addition, in the mid- to late seventeenth century, more families arrived from England, particularly from London and Dorsetshire (Dean 1831). Those in Scituate with Kentish heritage then no longer represented a significant proportion of the town's population. Hence, it is not surprising that the recessive disorders found on the Vineyard did not appear in the town's population.

22. Watertown in the 1630s was an extremely small community just outside of Boston. When I began my research on the early population of Martha's Vineyard, I mistakenly believed that a thorough knowledge of the ties within the Watertown group would establish the "founder" population. But the only definite English connection among members of the Watertown group was of three early residents who were from nearby villages in the county of Essex (Groce 1983:339). Circumstantial evidence indicates some prior connections in England among three more Vineyard settlers from Watertown, all of whom came to America on *The Elizabeth and Anne* in 1635. They may have been from the same area in England, but it is equally likely that they met on the voyage over and decided to settle near each other. It cannot even be stated with assurance that their decision to settle in Watertown was influenced by their traveling companions. Records indicate that a group of six or seven families also came to Martha's Vineyard from Hampton, New Hampshire, and

Kittery, Maine. These families, originally from Watertown, settled again among their former neighbors.

The first list of English origins of Edgartown proprietors, in 1653, shows a very diversified population:

Buckinghamshire, 1
Colchester, 1
Essex, 2
Kent (Ashford), 1
Lancashire, 1
London, 3
Middlesex, 1
Norwich, 2
Somersetshire, 1
Suffolk, 2
Wilts, 2
Unknown, 3

By the end of the seventeenth century there were at least three settlers (and four grown sons) from the Kentish Weald in Edgartown. The population as a whole, however, retained its original heterogeneity.

23. Once the first few Cape Cod settlers crossed Vineyard Sound to occupy land on this sparsely populated island, many followed to join family and friends. A network was established between the two areas, and family ties seem to have played an important role in moves from one community to another. Hence, many of those who arrived on the Vineyard in the later 1600s were already closely related to each other.

24. Of the remaining men, four were from families already established in Edgartown and one was from Braintree, near Boston. None had Kentish ancestors. The six men of Kent were from Sandwich, Barnstable, and Falmouth.

25. In 1694 there were eleven men with nine different surnames living in Chilmark. Five were from towns of the Kentish Weald. By the early 1700s three men had left the community, and there were only seven different surnames (although the number of household heads rose to fifteen). None of those who left were from Kent, so the percentage of Kentish surnames in the population rose from 45 percent to 56 percent.

26. Between 1700 and 1900, Vineyard families had an average of 6.61 children, but in the first generations of settlement the average was as high as 9.1 (Banks 1966). Families of ten to fifteen children were not uncommon, and more than twenty not unheard of (Daggett 1965).

27. Estimates of the early Island population and its distribution are often haphazard at best, but accuracy increases considerably by the mid-eighteenth century. Population estimates and colonial census records are available for

1641, 1653, 1660, 1670, 1676, 1680, 1692, 1694, 1699, 1700, 1742, and 1757. The first provincial census was taken in 1765, and the first federal census in 1790. In 1855 the federal census, taken at the start of each decade, was supplemented by a state census, taken in the middle of the decade.

4. The Genetics of Vineyard Deafness

1. Geneticists usually resort to a computer or to mathematical calculations to generate models of inbreeding or estimate numbers of carriers of a particular trait within a given population. The data from Martha's Vineyard, unfortunately, cannot be easily computerized or described. The population is simply too large and too highly inbred for current computer programs to deal with effectively. Moreover, we have no idea when the initial mutation occurred nor how inbred the community was *before* these people left England. Based solely on the relative numbers of individuals and their distribution in Kent prior to leaving for the New World, I would hazard a guess that the original individual in whom the mutation for deafness occurred lived in or near Ashford at least several generations before our group left for Scituate. My ongoing research may help to clarify the picture.

2. The population of Gay Head, on the extreme western end of the Island, consisted of remnants of the many different Indian groups that had once populated the entire Island. The Indians specialized in raising oxen before horses became the common animals for farm chores. For two hundred years Gay Head was officially part of the town of Chilmark, but the Indians maintained a distinct, cohesive community and had little to do with their white neighbors. In 1870 this separation was recognized officially, and Gay Head became an independent municipality. Today the town is one of only two predominantly Indian towns in Massachusetts. From the time of the earliest white settlement on the Island, there was some mating with the local Indian population, although there were few formal marriages between these two groups, and children of these unions were considered to be Indian rather than Yankee.

The Indian community managed to remain separate in large measure because of the geographic distance between the Indian and white settlements. There is little information on the ancestries of the Indian population. Banks's encyclopedic *History of Martha's Vineyard* was notably incomplete concerning later Indian history, and he provided no Indian genealogies. The Indian population was genetically far more heterogeneous than the nearby white population. The local Indians intermarried with Indians from the mainland, blacks, Brava Portuguese, and Portuguese.

No hereditary deafness was found in the Indian population, with the possible exception of one case in the early nineteenth century. In a book entitled *80*

Years Ashore and Afloat the narrator mentioned a "deaf and dumb negro," one of two men lost at sea in 1806 (Cornell 1873). Unfortunately, it is not known who this deaf man was. Although there is not enough evidence to include him in the list of those who had the inherited form of deafness, he cannot be excluded entirely from consideration. Islanders generally reserved the term "deaf and dumb" for those born deaf. The 1790 census listed 107 blacks, but this group was quickly absorbed into the Indian community, many of whom came to be considered "Negro" by the local Yankees. There was also a long tradition of Indian-white matings, however, so this "deaf and dumb" man might well have had several ancestors from the Kentish Weald.

3. Spuhler and Kluckhohn (1953) found that as much as 57 percent of the inbreeding in a Hopi community would be missed if one considered only those who married third cousins or closer. The hidden inbreeding would be between individuals who, though not recognized as cousins socially, shared an ancestor more distant than a great-great-grandfather.

4. Nineteenth-century references to intermarriage and resulting deafness on Martha's Vineyard include Ackers 1878:12; *American Annals of the Deaf* 1855; Bell 1886, 1891, 1892, 1969; Brooks 1855; Burnet 1835; Hartman 1881; Jenkins 1891; *Lancet*, Feb. 10, 1877; Miller 1895; and Withington 1885.

5. Despite the fact that Bell's memoir was published in 1883, it is still regularly cited. The conclusions Bell drew, that marriage between deaf individuals who have familial histories of deafness should be discouraged and that residential schools for the deaf should be abolished because these deaf might meet and marry there, are still mentioned. For example, a current, regularly republished textbook for audiologists cites Bell's work almost verbatim (Newby 1979:447). The Alexander Graham Bell Foundation, which is dedicated to the promulgation of speaking and lip reading among the deaf, recently reissued the text with only a brief foreword, in which the reader is told: "Many of Bell's perceptive insights and challenging questions merit the same careful consideration as if they had appeared in 1969 instead of 1883." Rightly or wrongly, Bell's research has become part of American deaf history. Individuals who want to determine whether they might have deaf children should be encouraged to seek out a competent medical geneticist. No responsible chemist, physicist, or biologist would rely on information published in 1883 without at least considering work done in the intervening years. The same should be true of human genetics.

5. The Island Adaptation to Deafness

1. This article, which I have not located, was published in one of the many Boston papers, probably between 1920 and 1923. Another informant recalled

that his mother was "awful mad" about an article, apparently the same one, in a Boston paper. It seems to have been very demeaning toward the Island's deaf inhabitants.

2. Research by Wilbur and Jones (1974) and Ahlgren (1977) indicates that manual dexterity develops in infants more rapidly than the ability to enunciate. Deaf infants and hearing infants of deaf parents apparently can begin to communicate in sign language several months earlier than the average hearing infant can begin to speak.

3. The laws of all the New England states allowed parents of deaf children to send their children either to schools that stressed oral communication (through lip reading), such as the Clarke Institute for the Deaf or the Horace Mann School in Boston, which opened in 1867, or to the American Asylum in Hartford, which used both sign language and in some instances lip reading (Gallaudet 1892). All deaf Vineyarders born after 1817 attended Hartford, but none seem to have been taught lip reading. Reading lips is an extremely difficult skill to acquire, taking years to learn. Even good lip readers tend to miss a significant amount of what is being said to them (Higgins 1980; Neisser 1983). Many intelligent deaf individuals find it simply impossible to follow a conversation by lip reading, preferring if at all possible to sign instead.

4. Beginning with the census of 1850, literacy and illiteracy were noted for all people over sixteen years of age. The only deaf individual listed as illiterate after education became available and common was a man who apparently was mentally ill and possibly mentally retarded. Even he had attended the Hartford school for a year.

5. Research indicates that those who are already competent in sign language have a tremendous head start in acquiring English (Schlesinger and Meadow 1972). To a native signer, of course, English is a second language. For the majority of those who are prelingually deafened, it remains a language used primarily for writing and reading.

6. Research on sign language is becoming increasingly sophisticated. See Stokoe 1972, 1980; Klima and Bellugi 1979; Schlesinger and Namir 1978; Siple 1978; and articles in the journal *Sign Language Studies*.

7. This early French sign system was apparently based on an indigenous sign language. Its invention has often been attributed to one of the giants of early deaf education—Abbé Charles-Michel de l'Epée, who established a school for the deaf in Paris in the 1760s. L'Epée himself made no such claims. He stated that he merely made more systematic or, as he said, "methodological" what seems to have been a regional sign language (Sallagoity 1975). For a discussion of the origins and history of French Sign Language, see Lane 1983.

8. Also see Frishberg 1975.

6. *Growing Up Deaf on the Vineyard*

1. Even after the establishment of state and private schools for the deaf, many children were kept at home because they were not near a school for the deaf or because they were needed on the farm or fishing vessel (Gordon 1892). Estimates varied on the numbers of deaf children who did not receive an education. According to the federal census of 1870, only 25 percent of deaf school-age children actually attended some educational institution (*Harper's* 1874). Noyes (1870) estimated that less than half of all deaf children in Minnesota were being educated, and Jenkins (1890b) believed the national figure to be closer to 69 percent.

The emphasis on deaf education on Martha's Vineyard was therefore unusually strong. In part this may have reflected the emphasis on education among the early settlers from Kent. Undoubtedly it reflected the local opinion that deaf children were intelligent, capable, and in need of the same education offered to other children if they were to take their rightful place in the community.

2. Bell (1892:20–21) found the percentage of deaf-deaf marriages rising steadily over the years, from 56 percent in 1810 to 81 percent in 1839 and 92 percent in 1860. Bell concluded by stating that "the percentage of deaf-hearing marriages is entirely insignificant now." Bell's sample was probably skewed, as he worked within the deaf community and had less contact with deaf people who did not participate in it. Nevertheless, this trend was also noted in Fay's (1898) demographic analysis of the American deaf population. The percentage of deaf Vineyarders who married other deaf individuals rose to 35 percent after the opening of the school in Hartford but was still significantly lower than on the mainland.

3. It was not uncommon for a Kentish yeoman's son to attend the local elementary school for a year or two (Chalkins 1970). This traditional emphasis on education continued in the New World.

4. Methodists did not believe in dancing, being particularly alarmed by the music and the bodily contact between the sexes. At Tucker parties, boys held girls by the hand rather than by the waist, and the music was restricted to respectable instruments such as the piano, rather than loud, sinful ensembles with fiddles. (The more devout did without instruments entirely.) An example of a Tucker party game is "Go In and Out the Window," which children still play. By the late nineteenth century, Methodist Tucker parties were just like Island house parties or "kitchen dances."

7. Deafness in Historical Perspective

1. For a more complete history of deaf education, see Davis and Silverman 1970; Di Carlo 1964; Lane 1983; and Savage et al. 1981.

2. In recent years many studies have been made of the deaf subculture, but to think of this subculture as a single entity is somewhat misleading. Certainly not all those who have a severe hearing loss consider themselves members. Conversely, some hearing individuals, because of marriage, family, or interest, are very active in it. The deaf subculture is extremely heterogeneous. Within the larger group there are distinct associations based on the degree of hearing loss, on education or occupation, and on racial, ethnic, religious, and sexual preferences. Among the most comprehensive sources are Higgins 1980; Jacobs 1974a, b; Johnson and Erting 1984; Markowicz and Woodward 1978; Meadow 1972; Padden and Markowicz 1975; Schein 1968; 1979.

Appendix B

1. *The American Annals of the Deaf and Dumb* was later changed to *The American Annals of the Deaf*.

Bibliography

Ackers, B. St. J. 1878. "The Causes of Deafness," *American Annals of the Deaf and Dumb* 23 (1): 10–17.

Adams, John. 1853. *The Life of "Reformation" John Adams, an elder of the Methodist Episcopal Church. Written by himself.* 2 vols. Boston: George C. Rand.

Ahlgren, I. 1977. Early Linguistic Cognitive Development in Deaf and Severely Hard of Hearing Children. Paper presented at the First National Symposium on Sign Language Research and Teaching, Chicago.

Allen, Joseph Chase. 1949. *Tales and Trails of Martha's Vineyard.* Boston: Little, Brown.

American Annals of the Deaf. 1890. "Miscellaneous: Marriages of the Deaf." 35 (3): 230–231.

American Annals of the Deaf and Dumb. 1848. "Miscellaneous: Numbers of the Deaf and Dumb." 1 (2): 131–132.

———— 1852. "Miscellaneous: Census of the Deaf and Dumb." 4 (4): 261–262.

———— 1852. "List of Pupils of the American Asylum from the Commencement of the Institution 1817, to May, 1851." 4 (4): 201–236.

———— 1855. "Intermarriage of Relatives." 8 (1): 60–61.

———— 1870a. "Miscellaneous: The Organ of the German Institutions." 15 (3): 186–187.

———— 1870b. "Miscellaneous: Deaf Mutes in the Time of Queen Elizabeth." 15 (3): 188–189.

———— 1873. "The Perversity of Deaf Mutism." 17 (3): 262–263.

———— 1874a. "Miscellaneous: Consanguinity of Parents." 19 (2):127–128.

———— 1874b. "Ninth Annual Report of the Board of State Charities of Massachusetts." Book review. 19 (2): 104–109.

American Asylum. 1837. *Twenty-First Annual Report of the Directors of the American Asylum at Hartford for the Education and Instruction of the Deaf and Dumb.* Hartford, Conn.: Hudson and Skinner.

—— 1861. *The Forty-Fifth Annual Report of the Directors of the American Asylum at Hartford for the Education and Instruction of the Deaf and Dumb.* Hartford, Conn.: Case, Lockwood.

Amman, John Conrad. [1700] 1873. *A Dissertation on Speech,* in which not only the Human Voice and the Art of Speaking are traced from their origin; But the means are also described by which those who have been deaf and dumb from their birth may acquire speech. Translated by John Baker. London: Sampson Low, Marston, Low, and Searle.

Anderson, T. Mc. 1863. "Hereditary Deaf-Mutism." *Medical Times and Gazette* (London) 2: 247.

Aulbers, B. J. M. 1959. *Erfelijke Aangeboren Doofheid in Zuid-Holland.* Delft: Waltman.

Banks, Charles. [1913] 1966. *The History of Martha's Vineyard,* 2d ed., vols. 1–3. Edgartown, Mass.: Dukes County Historical Society.

—— 1930. *The Planters of the Commonwealth.* Cambridge, Mass.: Riverside Press.

—— [1937] 1963. *Topographical Dictionary of 2885 English Emigrants to New England, 1620–1650,* 3d ed., ed. Elijah Ellsworth Brownell. Baltimore: Genealogical Publishing Co.

Barnard, P. 1834. "Education of the Deaf." *North American Review* 38 (83): 307–357.

Becker, Gaylene. 1980. *Growing Old in Silence.* Berkeley: University of California Press.

Bell, Alexander Graham. Manuscript. Alexander Graham Bell Family Papers (Container 187). Manuscript Division, Library of Congress, Washington, D.C.

—— Manuscript. Alexander Graham Bell's Papers. Manuscripts and unbound notes. John Hitz Memorial Library, Alexander Graham Bell Association for the Deaf, Washington, D.C.

—— [1883] 1969. *Memoir Upon the Formation of a Deaf Variety of the Human Race.* Washington: Alexander Graham Bell Association for the Deaf.

—— 1885. "Is There a Correlation between Defects of the Senses?" *Science* 5 (106): 127–129.

—— 1886. "The Deaf-Mutes of Martha's Vineyard." *American Annals of the Deaf* 31 (3): 282–284.

—— 1888. *Facts and Opinions Relating to the Deaf from America.* London: Spottiswoode.

——— 1891. "Marriage: An Address Delivered to the Members of the Literary Society of Kendall Green, Washington, D.C., March 6, 1891." *Science* 17 (424): 160–163.

——— 1892. "Testimony of Alexander Graham Bell." In *Education of Deaf Children,* ed. Joseph C. Gordon. Washington, D.C.: Volta Bureau.

——— 1899. "A Philanthropist of the Last Century Identified as a Boston Man." *Proceedings of the American Antiquarian Society* 13: 383–393.

——— 1913. Letter from Alexander Graham Bell to Mr. F. Deland of the Volta Bureau, July 16, 1913. Bell Family Papers (Container 187). Manuscript Division, Library of Congress, Washington, D.C.

Bell, John. 1859. "The Effects of the Consanguinity of Parents Upon the Mental Constitution of the Offspring." *Boston Medical and Surgical Journal* 61: 473–484.

Bellugi, Ursula. 1972. "Studies in Sign Language." In *Psycholinguistics and Total Communication: The State of the Art,* ed. Terrence O'Rourke. Washington, D.C.: American Annals of the Deaf, pp. 68–84.

Bellugi, Ursula, and Susan Fischer. 1972. "A Comparison of Sign Language and Spoken Language." *Cognition: International Journal of Cognitive Psychology* 1: 173–200.

Bellugi, Ursula, and E. Klima. 1975. "Aspects of Sign Language and Its Structure." In *The Role of Speech in Language,* ed. James F. Kavanagh and James E. Cutting. Cambridge, Mass.: MIT Press, pp. 171–205.

Bemiss, S. M. 1858. "Report on the Influence of Marriages of Consanguinity upon Offspring." *Transactions of the American Medical Association,* minutes of the 11th annual meeting 2: 319–425.

Bender, R. 1970. *The Conquest of Deafness.* Cleveland: Case Western Reserve.

Bignell, Alan. 1975. *Kent Villages.* London: Robert Hale.

Biklen, Douglas P. 1975. "Deaf Children vs the Board of Education." *American Annals of the Deaf* 120 (4): 382–386.

Birdsell, J. D. 1972. *Human Evolution: An Introduction to the New Physical Anthropology.* Chicago: Rand McNally.

Booth, Edmund. 1858. "Mr. Flournoy's Project." *American Annals of the Deaf and Dumb* 10 (1): 72–79.

Boston Medical and Surgical Journal. 1859. "Marriages of Consanguinity." July 28.

Boston Sunday Herald. 1895. "Mark of Chilmark, Deaf and Dumb in the Village of Squibnocket." Jan. 20.

Boyce, A. J., C. F. Küchemann, and G. A. Harrison. 1967a. "Neighborhood Knowledge and the Distribution of Marriage Distances." *Annals of Human Genetics* 30: 335–338.

——— 1967b. "The Reconstruction of Historical Movement Patterns."

In *Record Linkage in Medicine,* ed. E. D. Acheson. London: E. S. Livingston.

Brill, Richard G. 1975. "Mainstreaming: Format or Quality?" *American Annals of the Deaf* 120 (4): 377–381.

Bronstein, Harry. 1978. "Sign Language in the Education of the Deaf." In *Sign Language of the Deaf,* ed. L. M. Schlesinger and L. Namir. New York: Academic Press.

Brooks, Charles. 1856. "Laws of Reproduction, Considered with Particular Reference to the Intermarriage of First-Cousins." *Proceedings of the American Academy for the Advancement of Science.* Cambridge, Mass.: Joseph Lovering.

Brown, Roger. 1977. "Why Are Signed Languages Easier to Learn than Spoken Languages?" Paper presented to the First National Symposium on Sign Language Research and Teaching, Chicago.

Bruce, Robert V. 1973. *Alexander Graham Bell and the Conquest of Solitude.* Boston: Little, Brown.

Bulwer, John. 1648. *Philocophus: Or the Deafe and Dumbe Mans Friend.* London: Humphrey Moseley.

Burnet, John R. 1835. *Tales of the Deaf and Dumb.* Newark, N.J.: Benjamin Olds.

Camp, Henry B. 1848. "Claims of the Deaf and Dumb upon Public Sympathy and Aid." *American Annals of the Deaf and Dumb* 1 (4): 210–214.

Carlin, John. 1851. "Advantages and Disadvantages of the Use of Sign Language." *American Annals of the Deaf and Dumb* 4 (1): 49–57.

Chalkins, C. W. 1965. *Seventeenth Century Kent.* London: Longmans Green.

Chamberlain, William W. 1857. "Proceedings of the Convention of the New England Gallaudet Association of Deaf-Mutes." *American Annals of the Deaf and Dumb* 9 (2): 62–87.

Chapman, A. C., and A. M. Jacquard. 1971. "Un isolate d'Amerique Centrale: les Indiens Jicques de Honduras" in *Genetique et Population: Hommage a Jean Sutter.* Paris: I.N.E.D., pp. 163–185.

Chung, C. S., and K. S. Brown. 1970. "Family Studies of Early Childhood Deafness Ascertained through the Clark School for the Deaf." *American Journal of Human Genetics* 22: 630–644.

Chung, C. S., O. W. Robinson, and N. E. Morton. 1959. "A Note on Deaf-Mutism." *Annals of Human Genetics* 23: 357–366.

Cicourel, Aaron V., and Robert J. Boese. 1972. "Sign Language Acquisition and the Teaching of Deaf Children," pt. 2. *American Annals of the Deaf* 117 (3): 403–411.

Clark, Peter. 1977. *English Provincial Society from the Reformation to the*

Revolution: Religion, Politics and Society in Kent, 1500–1640. Hassocks, Sussex: Harvester Press.

Clerc, Laurent. 1818. *Address Read at a Public Examination of the Pupils in the Connecticut Asylum*. Hartford, Conn.: Hudson.

Cogswell, Leander W. [1880] 1973. *History of the Town of Henniker, Merrimack County, New Hampshire*. Somersworth, N.H.: New Hampshire Publishing.

Cornell, E. C. 1873. *Eighty Years Ashore and Afloat: Or the Thrilling Adventure of Uncle Jethro*. Boston: Andrew F. Graves.

Costeff, Hanan, and Hanna Dar. 1980. "Consanguinity Analysis of Congenital Deafness in Northern Israel." *American Journal of Human Genetics* 32: 64–68.

Cottage City Star (Oak Bluffs, Mass.). 1881. "Drowning Accident."

Covington, V. C. 1980. "Problems of Acculturation into the Deaf Community." *Sign Language Studies* 28: 267–285.

Cranefield, Paul F., and Walter Federn. 1970. "Paulus Zacchias on Mental Deficiency and on Deafness." *Bulletin of the New York Academy of Medicine* 46 (1): 3–21.

Crèvecoeur, Michel de. [1782] 1957. *Letters from an American Farmer*. New York: E. P. Dutton.

Croneberg, C. 1976. "Sign Language Dialects." In *A Dictionary of American Sign Language on Linguistic Principles*, new ed., ed. W. Stokoe, D. Casterline, and C. Croneberg. Silver Spring, Md.: Linstock Press.

Daggett, John Tobey. 1965. *It Began with a Whale: Memories of Cedar Tree Neck, Martha's Vineyard*. Somerville, Mass.: Fleming and Sons.

Dalgarno, George. (1680) 1971. *Didascalocophus or the Deaf and Dumb Mans Tutor*. Menston, Eng.: Scholar Press.

Damon, Daniel E. 1884. "History of Scituate and South Scituate." In *History of Plymouth County, Massachusetts,"* ed. D. Hamilton Hurd. Philadelphia: J. W. Lewis.

Darwin, Charles. (1868) 1920. *The Variation of Animals and Plants under Domestication*. New York: Appleton.

David, J. B., B. B. Edoo, J. F. O. Mustaffah, and R. Hinchcliff. 1971. "Adamarobe—a 'Deaf' Village." *Sound* 5: 70.

Davis, Fred. 1961. "Deviance Disavowal: The Management of Strained Interaction by the Visibly Handicapped." *Social Problems* 9: 120–132.

Davis, Hallowell, and S. Richard Silverman. 1970. *Hearing and Deafness*, 3d ed. New York: Holt, Rinehart and Winston.

Deane, Samuel. 1831. *History of the Town of Scituate*. Boston: James Loring.

Demos, John. 1970. *A Little Commonwealth*. New York: Oxford University Press.

Deuchar, Margaret. 1977. "Sign Language Diglossia in a British Deaf Community." *Sign Language Studies* 17: 347–356.

Devon, Samuel Adams. 1838. *Sketches of Martha's Vineyard and Other Reminiscences.* Boston: James Monroe.

Deyo, Simeon L., ed. 1890. *History of Barnstable County, Massachusetts.* New York: H. W. Blake.

Di Carlo, Louis M. 1964. *The Deaf.* Englewood Cliffs, N.J.: Prentice-Hall.

Doran, Edwin, Jr. 1952. "Inbreeding in an Isolated Island Community." *Journal of Heredity* 43: 263–266.

Douglas, Mary. 1966. *Purity and Danger.* New York: Praeger.

Dudley, A. J. F. 1973. "Four Kent Towns at the End of the Middle Ages." In *Essays in Kentish History,* ed. Roake and Whyman. London: Frank Cass, pp. 61–74.

Edgerton, Robert. 1967. *The Cloake of Competence.* Berkeley: University of California Press.

——— 1970. "Mental Retardation in Non-Western Societies: Toward a Cross-Cultural Perspective on Incompetence." In *Social-Cultural Aspects of Mental Retardation,* Proceedings of the Peabody-NIMH Conference, ed. H. Carl Haywood. New York: Appleton-Century Crofts.

——— 1976. *Deviance: A Cross-Cultural Perspective.* Menlo Park, Calif.: Cummings Press.

Eldridge, G. W. 1889. *Martha's Vineyard: Its History and Its Advantages as a Health Resort.* Providence, R.I.: Freeman and Sons.

Elvin, Joseph B. 1963. "The Lamberts Cove Cemetery." *Dukes County Intelligencer* 5 (2).

Emery, Philip A. 1884. *A Plea for Early Mute Education, Deaf-Mute Day Schools and the Objections to them Answered,* pamphlet no. 1, Chicago Day Schools.

Everitt, Alan M. 1956. *The County Committee of Kent in the Civil War.* University College of Leicester, Department of English Local History, Occasional Paper no. 9. Leicester, Eng.: Broadwater Press.

——— 1966. *The Community of Kent and the Great Rebellion, 1640–1660.* Leicester, Eng.: Leicester University Press.

Fay, Edward A. 1876. "Consanguineous Marriages as a Cause of Deaf-Mutism." *American Annals of the Deaf and Dumb* 21 (4): 204–216.

——— 1888. "Deaf-Mutes." *American Annals of the Deaf* 33 (3): 199–216; 33 (4): 241–259.

——— 1898. *Marriages of the Deaf in America.* Washington, D.C.: Volta Bureau.

Feldman, H., Goldin-Meadow, S., and Gleitman, L. 1978. "Beyond Heroditus: The Creation of Language by Linguistically Deprived Deaf Children."

In *Action, Gesture and Symbol,* ed. A. Locke. New York: Academic Press.

Fischer, Susan. 1978. "Sign Language and Creoles." In *Understanding Language through Sign Language Research,* ed. P. Siple. New York: Academic Press, pp. 309–331.

Fraser, George R. 1964. "Profound Childhood Deafness." *Journal of Medical Genetics* 1: 118–151.

———— 1976. *The Causes of Profound Deafness in Childhood.* Baltimore: Johns Hopkins University Press.

Freeman, Fredrick. 1862. *The History of Cape Cod,* vols. 1 and 2. Boston.

Freeman, James. 1971. "Dukes County, 1807." *Dukes County Intelligencer* 12 (4).

Frishberg, Nancy. 1975. "Arbitrariness and Iconicity: Historical Change in American Sign Language." *Language* 51: 696–719.

———— 1978. "Code and Culture." In *Sign Language and Language Acquisition in Man and Ape,* ed. F. C. Peng. Colorado: Westview Press.

Furley, Robert. 1871. *A History of the Weald of Kent,* vols. 1 and 2. Ashford: Henry Iggleden.

Furusho, T. 1957. "A Genetic Study on the Congenital Deafness." *Japanese Journal of Human Genetics* 2: 35.

Gallaudet, Edward M. 1886. "History of Deaf-Mute Education in the United States." *American Annals of the Deaf and Dumb* 31 (2): 130–147.

———— 1890. "The Intermarriage of the Deaf and Their Education." *Science* 16 (408): 295–299.

———— 1892. "The Testimony of Edward Minor Gallaudet." In *The Education of Deaf Children,* ed. J. C. Gordon. Washington, D.C.: Volta Bureau.

Galton, Francis. 1885. "Hereditary Deafness." *Nature* 31: 269–270.

Gillett, Philip G. 1890. "Deaf-Mutes." *Science* 16 (404): 248–249.

———— 1891. "Deaf-Mutes: Their Intermarriages and Offspring." *Science* 17 (417): 57–60.

Glass, Bentley. 1953. "The Genetics of the Dunkers." *Scientific American* 189 (2): 76–81.

Glass, B., M. Sacks, E. Jahn, and C. Hess. 1952. "Genetic Drift in a Religious Isolate, an Analysis of the Causes of Variation in Blood Groups and Other Gene Frequencies in a Small Population." *American Naturalist* 86 (828): 145–159.

Gliedman, John, and William Roth. 1980. *The Unexpected Minority: Handicapped Children in America.* New York: Harcourt Brace Jovanovich.

Goffman, E. 1963. *Stigma: Notes on the Management of Spoiled Identity.* Englewood Cliffs, N.J.: Prentice-Hall.

Goldin-Meadow, S., and H. Feldman. 1977. "The Development of Language-like Communication without a Language Model." *Science* 165: 664–672.

Gordon, Joseph C. 1892. *Education of Deaf Children: Evidence of Edward Minor Gallaudet and Alexander Graham Bell presented to the Royal Commission of the United Kingdom on the Condition of the Blind, the Deaf and Dumb, etc.* Washington, D.C.: Volta Bureau.

Green, Samuel. 1861. "The Earliest Advocate of the Education of Deaf Mutes in America." *American Annals of the Deaf and Dumb* 13 (1): 1–8.

Greene, Lawrence S. 1973. "Physical Growth and Development, Neurological Maturation and Behavioral Functioning in Two Ecuadorian Andean Communities in Which Goiter Is Endemic." *American Journal of Physical Anthropology* 38: 119–134.

—— 1977. "Hyperendemic Goiter, Cretinism, and Social Organization in Highland Ecuador." In *Malnutrition, Behavior and Social Organization,* ed. Lawrence S. Greene. New York: Academic Press.

Green, Philip J. Jr. 1970. *Four Generations: Population, Land and Family in Colonial Andover, Massachusetts.* Ithaca, N.Y.: Cornell University Press.

Groce, Nora, E. 1980. "Everyone Here Spoke Sign Language." *Natural History* 89 (6): 6–12.

—— 1981. "The Island's Hereditary Deafness: A Lesson in Human Understanding." *Dukes County Intelligencer* 22 (3).

—— 1982. "The American Deaf Community in an Historical Perspective." In *The Deaf Community and the Deaf Population,* ed. Higgins and Nash. Monograph no. 3 in The Sociology of the Deaf. Washington: Gallaudet University Press.

—— 1983. Hereditary Deafness on the Island of Martha's Vineyard: The Ethnohistory of a Genetic Disorder. Ph.D. dissertation, Brown University.

Gutman, Robert. 1958. "Birth and Death Registration in Massachusetts: The Colonial Period, 1639–1800." *Milbank Memorial Fund Quarterly* 36 (1): 58–74.

Gwaltney, John L. 1970. *The Thrice Shy.* New York: Columbia University Press.

Hagaman, Roberta M., Walter S. Elias, and Robert M. Netting. 1978. "The Genetic and Demographic Impact of In-migrants in a Largely Endogamous Community." *Annals of Human Biology* 5 (6).

Hand, Wayland D. 1980. "Deformity, Disease and Physical Ailment as Divine Retribution." In *Magical Medicine.* Berkeley: University of California Press, pp. 57–67.

Hanhart, E. 1962. "Die genealogische und otologische Erforschung des grossen Walliser Herdes von rezessiver Taubheit und Schwerhörigkeit im Laufe der letzten 30 Jahre (1933–1962)." *Arch. Klaus-Stift Vererb-Forsch* 37: 199.

Hanks, Jane R., and L. M. Hanks, Jr. 1948. "The Physically Handicapped in Certain Non-Occidental Societies." *Journal of Social Issues* 4: 11–20.

Harper's New Monthly Magazine. 1874. "The Defective Class." 68: 735–739.

Hartman, Arthur. 1881. *Deaf Mutes and the Education of Deaf Mutes by Lip Reading and Articulation.* London: Bailliere, Tindall and Cox Parc.

Hasted, Edward. 1797. *The History and Topographical Survey of the County of Kent,* vol. 1. Canterbury: W. Bristow.

Hawkins, James. 1863. *The Physical, Moral and Intellectual Constitution of the Deaf and Dumb.* London: Longman, Green, Longman, Roberts and Green.

Higgins, Paul C. 1980. *Outsiders in a Hearing World: A Society of Deafness.* Beverly Hills, Calif.: Sage Press.

Higgins, Paul C., and Jeff Nash, eds. 1982. *The Deaf Community and the Deaf Population.* Monograph no. 3. Washington, D.C.: Gallaudet College Press.

Homes, William. 1715–1747. Journal of Rev. Wm. Homes of Londonderry, Ireland and Chilmark, Martha's Vineyard. Manuscript. Maine Historical Society, Portland, Me.

Hough, Henry Beetle. 1936. *Martha's Vineyard, Summer Resort, 1835–1935.* Rutland, Vt.: Tuttle.

Huntington, E. Gale. 1957. *Songs the Whalemen Sang.* Barre, Mass.: Barre Press.

——— 1966. "Folksongs from Martha's Vineyard." *Northeast Folklore,* vol. 8. Orono, Me.

——— 1969. *An Introduction to Martha's Vineyard.* Edgartown, Mass.: Dukes County Historical Society.

——— 1975. "Nomansland, Salt Cod and the Nomansland Boat." *Dukes County Intelligencer* 17 (1): 51–71.

Huth, Alfred Henry. 1878. "Consanguineous Marriages." *American Annals of the Deaf and Dumb* 23 (2): 144–150.

Ives, Edward D. 1980. *The Tape Recorded Interview.* Knoxville: University of Tennessee Press.

Jacobs, J. A. 1869. "Dummies." *American Annals of the Deaf and Dumb* 14 (1): 20–23.

Jacobs, Leo. 1974a. "The Community of the Adult Deaf." *American Annals of the Deaf* 119 (1): 41–46.

——— 1974b. *A Deaf Adult Speaks Out.* Washington, D.C.: Gallaudet College Press.

Jenkins, William G. 1890a. "The Scientific Testimony of 'Facts and Opinions.'" *American Annals of the Deaf* 35 (3): 184–191.

—— 1890b. "Professor A. Graham Bell's Studies on the Deaf." *Science* 16 (395): 117–119.

—— 1891. "Heredity in Its Relation to Deafness." *American Annals of the Deaf* 36 (2): 97–111.

Jerrold, Walter. 1907. *Highways and Byways in Kent*. London: Macmillan.

Johnson, Robert E., and Carol Erting. 1984. *Linguistic Socialization in the Context of Emergent Deaf Ethnicity*. Working Papers in Anthropology. New York: Wenner Gren Foundation.

Kendon, A. 1980. "A Description of a Deaf-Mute Sign Language from the Enga Province of Papua New Guinea with Some Comparative Discussion." *Semiotica* 3 (1–2): 1–34.

Kilburne, Richard. 1659. *A Topographic Survey of the County of Kent with some Chronological, Historical, and other Matters touching the Same*. London: Thomas Mabb.

Kingesbury, Samuel. Manuscript. Records of Deaths Kept by Rev. Samuel Kingesbury, minister in Edgartown. Dukes County Historical Society Library, Box 95B.

Klima, Edward, and Ursula Bellugi. 1979. *The Signs of Language*. Cambridge, Mass.: Harvard University Press.

Konigsmark, Bruce W. 1969. "Hereditary Deafness in Man." *New England Journal of Medicine* 281: 713–720, 774–778, 827–832.

—— 1972. "Genetic Hearing Loss with No Associated Abnormalities." *Journal of Speech and Hearing Disorders* 37: 89–99.

Konigsmark, Bruce W., and Robert J. Gorlin. 1976. *Genetic and Metabolic Deafness*. Philadelphia: W. B. Saunders.

Kuchemann, C. F., A. J. Boyce, and G. A. Harrison. 1967. "A Demographic and Genetic Study of a Group of Oxfordshire Villages." *Human Biology* 39 (3): 251–279.

Kurath, Hans. 1970. *A Word Geography of the Eastern United States*, 4th ed. Ann Arbor: University of Michigan Press.

Kuschel, Rolf. 1973. "The Silent Inventor: The Creation of a Sign Language by the Only Deaf-Mute on a Polynesian Island." *Sign Language Studies* 3: 1–28.

—— 1974. "A Lexicon of Signs from a Polynesian Outlier Island: A Description of 217 Signs as Developed and Used by Kangobai, the only Deaf-Mute of Rennell Island." *Psykologick Skriftserie* no. 8. Copenhagen: Copenhagen University.

Labov, William. 1972. "The Social Motivation of a Sound Change." *Sociolinguistic Patterns*. Philadelphia: University of Pennsylvania Press.

Lancet. 1887. "Miscellaneous." Feb. 10.

Lane, Harlan, ed. 1984. *The Deaf Experience*. Cambridge, Mass.: Harvard University Press.

Laslett, Peter. 1948. "The Gentry of Kent in 1640." *Cambridge Historical Journal* 9: 148–164.

Laslett, Peter, and Peter Harrison. 1963. "Clayworth and Cogenhoe." In *Historical Essays, 1660–1750, Presented to David Ogg,* ed. H. E. Bell and R. L. Ollard. London: Black.

Livingston, Frank B. 1969. "The Founder Effect and Deleterious Genes." *American Journal of Physical Anthropology* 30: 55–59.

Lockridge, Kenneth A. 1966. "The Population of Dedham, Massachusetts, 1636–1736." *The Economic History Review* 19 (2): 318–344.

———— 1970. *A New England Town: The First Hundred Years.* New York: W. W. Norton.

Lord, Annie Daggett. 1964. "The Language of Martha's Vineyard." *Dukes County Intelligencer* 6 (2).

Luce, L. 1885. Letter from L. Luce to Dr. C. F. Withington, May 18, 1885. Alexander Graham Bell Papers, John Hitz Memorial Library, Alexander Graham Bell Foundation, Washington, D.C.

Majumdar, M. K. 1972. "Preliminary Study on Consanguinity and Deaf Mutes." *Journal of the Indian Medical Association* 58: 78.

Mann, Edwin J. 1836. *The Deaf and Dumb or, A collection of Articles Relating to the Condition of Deaf-Mutes, their Education and the Principal Asylums Devoted to Their Instruction.* Boston: D. K. Hitchcock.

Markowicz, Harry. 1972. "Some Sociolinguistic Considerations of American Sign Language." *Sign Language Studies* 1: 15–41.

Markowicz, Harry, and James C. Woodward. 1978. "Language and Maintenance of Ethnic Boundaries in the Deaf Community." *Communication and Cognition* 2: 29–38.

Mayberry, Rachel I. 1978. "French-Canadian Sign Language: A Study of Inter-Sign Language Comprehension." In *Understanding Language through Sign Language Research,* ed. Patricia Siple. New York: Academic Press.

Mayhew, Eleanor Ransom, ed. 1956. *Martha's Vineyard: A Short History.* Edgartown, Mass.: Dukes County Historical Society.

———— 1959. "The Christiantown Story 1659–1959." *Dukes County Intelligencer* 1 (1).

McKusick, Victor A. 1978. *Medical Genetic Studies of the Amish: Selected Papers.* Baltimore: Johns Hopkins University Press.

McManis, Douglas. 1975. *Colonial New England: A Historical Geography.* New York: Oxford University Press.

Meadow, Kathryn P. 1968. "Early Manual Communicator in Relation to the Deaf Child's Intellectual, Social and Communicative Functioning." *American Annals of the Deaf* 113 (1): 29–41.

———— 1972. "Sociolinguistics, Sign Language and the Deaf Sub-Culture." In *Psycholinguistics and Total Communication: The State of the Art,* ed. T. J. O'Rourke. Washington, D.C.: American Annals of the Deaf, pp. 19–37.

Mengel, M. C., B. W. Konigsmark, C. I. Berlin, and V. A. McKusick. 1967. "Recessive Early-Onset Neural Deafness." *Acta Oto-laryngologica* 64: 313–326.

Menière, P. 1846. "Recherches sur l'origine de la Surdi-Mutité." *Gazette de Médicine* (Paris) ser. 3 (1): 223–243.

————— 1856. "Du Mariage entre parents considéré comme cause de la surdi-mutité congénitale." *Gazette de Médicine,* ser. 3 (2): 303.

Miller, S. Millington. 1895. "The Ascent of Man." *Arena* 12: 130–135.

Mindel, E. D., and M. Vernon. 1971. *They Grow in Silence.* Silver Spring, Md.: National Association for the Deaf.

Mitchell, Arthur. 1863. "Interesting Case of Hereditary Deaf-Mutism." *Medical Times and Gazette* 2: 164.

Mitchell, Sue H. 1971. "The Haunting Influence of Alexander Graham Bell." *American Annals of the Deaf.* 116: (3): 349–356.

Morgan, Edward S. 1966. *The Puritan Family.* New York: Harper and Row.

Morris, O. W. 1861. "Consanguineous Marriages and Their Results in Respect to Deaf-Dumbness." *American Annals of the Deaf and Dumb* 13 (1): 29–35.

Morton, Newton E. 1960. "The Mutational Load Due to Detrimental Genes in Man." *American Journal of Human Genetics* 12: 348–364.

Nash, Jeffrey E., and Anedith Nash. 1981. *Deafness in Society.* Lexington, Mass.: D. C. Heath.

National Center for Health Statistics. 1982. "Hearing Ability of Persons by Sociodemographic and Health Characteristics, United States." *Vital and Health Statistics,* ser. 10, no. 140, August. Washington, D.C.

Neal, Daniel. 1754. *The History of the Puritans, or of the Protestant Non-conformists, from the Reformation under King Henry VIII to the Act of Toleration under King William and Queen Mary,* 2d ed., vol. 1. London: J. Buckland.

Neel, James U. 1970. "Lessons from a 'Primitive' People." *Science* 170: 815–822.

Neisser, Arden. 1983. *The Other Side of Silence.* New York: Alfred A. Knopf.

Newby, Hayes A. 1979. *Audiology,* 4th ed. Englewood Cliffs, N.J.: Prentice-Hall.

Newman, Lucile F. 1969. "Folklore of Pregnancy: Wives' Tales in Contra Costa County, California." *Western Folklore* 28 (2): 112–135.

Norton, Henry Franklin. 1923. *Martha's Vineyard, the Story of Its Towns.* Hartford, Conn.: Pyne Printery.

Norton, Roy. Norton Genealogical File. Manuscript. Dukes County Historical Society, Edgartown, Mass.

Noyes, J. L. 1870. "Compulsory Education as Applied to Deaf-Mutes." *American Annals of the Deaf and Dumb* 15 (4): 216–223.

Opren, Charles Edward Herbert. 1836. *Anecdotes and Annals of the Deaf and Dumb*, 2d ed. London: Robert H. C. Tims.

Otis, Amos. 1888. *Genealogical Notes of Barnstable Families,* ed. Charles Swift. Barnstable, Mass.: F. B. and F. P. Gross.

—— 1914. "The Lumbert or Lombard Family." *Library of Cape Cod History and Genealogy* no. 54. Yarmouth, Mass.: C. W. Swift.

Padden, Carol. 1980. "The Deaf Community and the Culture of Deaf People." In *Sign Language and the Deaf Community,* ed. C. Baker and R. Battison. Silver Spring, Md.: National Association of the Deaf, pp. 80–103.

Padden, Carol, and Markowicz, H. 1975. "Cultural Conflicts between Hearing and Deaf Communities." In *Proceedings of the Seventh World Congress of the World Federation of the Deaf.* Silver Spring, Md.: National Association of the Deaf, pp. 407–411.

Pease, Jeremiah. 1974. "Excerpts from Jeremiah Pease's Diary from the Archives." *Dukes County Intelligencer* 16 (2): 39–51.

Pease, Richard L. 1883. Letter from Richard L. Pease to Peter Thatcher Esqr.: Jan. 23. Alexander Graham Bell Papers, John Hitz Memorial Library, Alexander Graham Bell Foundation, Washington, D.C.

—— 1888a. Letter from Richard L. Pease to Mr. John Hitz, Edgartown, Mass., Feb. 18. Alexander Graham Bell Papers, John Hitz Memorial Library, Alexander Graham Bell Foundation.

—— 1888b. Letter from Richard L. Pease to Alexander Graham Bell. Alexander Graham Bell Family Papers, Manuscript Division, Library of Congress, Washington, D.C.

Peet, Dudley. 1856. "The Remote and Proximate Causes of Deafness" *American Annals of the Deaf and Dumb* 8 (3): 129–158.

Peet, Harvey P. 1851. "Analysis of Bonet's Treatise on the Art of Teaching the Dumb to Speak." *American Annals of the Deaf and Dumb* 3 (4): 200–211.

—— 1852. "Statistics of the Deaf and Dumb." *American Annals of the Deaf and Dumb* 5 (1): 1–21.

—— 1854. "List of the Pupils of the New York Institution for the Instruction of the Deaf and Dumb." *American Annals of the Deaf and Dumb* 6 (4): 193–241.

Peet, Issac Lewis. 1851. "Moral State of the Deaf and Dumb Previous to Education, and the Means and Results of Religious Influence Among Them." *American Annals of the Deaf and Dumb* 3 (4): 211–216.

—— 1872. "The Physical Status and Criminal Responsibility of the Totally Uneducated Deaf and Dumb." *American Annals of the Deaf and Dumb* 17 (2): 65–94.

Peltz, William L. 1972. *Saltwater in My Veins: Tales by Capt. Norman Benson, Trap Fisherman of Martha's Vineyard*. West Tisbury, Mass.: Vineyard Press.

Peng, Fred C., ed. 1974. "Kinship Signs in Japanese Sign Language." *Sign Language Studies* 5: 31–47.

———— 1978. *Sign Language and Language Acquisition in Man and Ape: New Dimensions in Comparative Pedolinguistics*. Boulder, Colo.: Westview Press.

Poole, Dorothy Cottle. 1976. *A New Vineyard*. Edgartown, Mass.: Dukes County Historical Society.

Porter, Samuel. 1854. "A Contrast." *American Annals of the Deaf and Dumb* 7 (1): 15–19.

Powell, Chilton L. 1928. "Marriages in Early New England." *New England Quarterly* 1: 323–334.

Pratt, Annie. n.d. Collection of manuscripts and notes gathered for Research of Alexander Graham Bell. Dukes County Historical Society Library, Edgartown, Mass.

Pratt, Harvey Hunter. 1929. *The Early Planters of Scituate*. Scituate, Mass.: Scituate Historical Society.

Prinz, Philip M., and Elisabeth A. Prinz. 1979. "Simultaneous Acquisition of ASL and Spoken English." *Sign Language Studies* 25: 283–296.

———— 1980. "Acquisition of ASL and Spoken English by a Hearing Child of a Deaf Mother and a Hearing Father." *Sign Language Studies* 30: 78–88.

Puybonnieux, J. B. 1846. *Mutisme et Surdité ou l'Influence de la Surdité Native sur les Facultés Physiques, Intellectuelles et Morales*. Paris: Ballière.

Rainer, John D., and Kenneth Altschuler, eds. 1968. *Psychiatry and the Deaf*. U.S. Department of Health, Education and Welfare: Social and Rehabilitation Service.

Rainer, John D., Kenneth Altschuler, and Franz J. Kallmann, eds. 1963. *Family and Mental Health Problems in a Deaf Population*. New York: Department of Medical Genetics, Columbia University.

Redden, Laura. 1858. "A Few Words about the Deaf and Dumb." *American Annals of the Deaf and Dumb* 10 (3): 177–181.

Ritchie, William A. 1969. *The Archaeology of Martha's Vineyard*. New York: Natural History Press.

Romeo, Luigi. 1978. "For a Medieval History of Gesture Communication." *Sign Language Studies* 28: 353–380.

Rutman, Darrett B. 1965. *Winthrop's Boston: A Portrait of a Puritan Town, 1630–1649*. New York: W. W. Norton.

Sallagoity, Pierre. 1975. "The Sign Language of Southern France." *Sign Language Studies* 7: 181–202.

Sanborn, F. B. 1884. Letter from F. B. Sanborn, Office of Inspector of Charities, Board of Health, Lunacy and Charity, to Alexander Graham Bell, Aug. 28. Alexander Graham Bell Family Papers, Container 187, Manuscript Division, Library of Congress, Washington, D.C.

Sank, D. 1963. "The Genetic Aspects of Early Total Deafness." In *Family and Mental Health Problems in the Deaf Population,* ed. Rainer, Altschuler, Kallman, and Deming. New York: Columbia University Press.

Savage, R. D., L. Evans, and J. F. Savage. 1981. *Psychology and Communication in Deaf Children.* Sydney, Australia: Grune and Stratton.

Schein, Jerome D. 1968. *The Deaf Community: Studies in the Social Psychology of Deafness.* Washington, D.C.: Gallaudet College Press.

———— 1979. "Society and Culture of Hearing-Impaired People." In *Hearing and Hearing Impairments,* ed. Bradford and Hardy. New York: Grune and Stratton, pp. 479–487.

Schein, Jerome, and M. Delk. 1974. *The Deaf Population of the United States.* Silver Spring, Md.: National Association of the Deaf.

Schlesinger, Hilde S., and Kathryn P. Meadow. 1972. *Sound and Sign: Childhood Deafness and Mental Health.* Berkeley: University of California Press.

Schlesinger, L. M., and Lila Namir, eds. 1978. *Sign Language of the Deaf: Psychological, Linguistic and Sociological Perspectives.* New York: Academic Press.

Scott, W. R. 1870. *The Deaf and Dumb,* 2d ed. London: Bell and Daldy.

Seaver, Paul S. 1976. *Seventeenth-Century Kent.* New York: Franklin Watts.

Secrétan, J. P. 1954. "De la surdi-mutité récessive et de ses rapports avec les autres formes de surti-mutité." *Arch. Klaus-Stift Vererb-Forsch.* 29 (1).

Sedgwick, William. 1861. "On Sexual Limitation in Hereditary Disease." *British Foreign Medical and Chirugical Review* 28: 198–214.

Seiss, Joseph A. 1887. *The Children of Silence or, the Story of the Deaf.* Philadelphia: Porter and Coates.

Sewell, Samuel. 1972. *Diary of Samuel Sewell, 1674–1729,* vol. 2. New York: Arno Press.

Shuman, Malcolm K. 1980a. "Culture and Deafness in Maya Indian Society: An Examination of Illness Roles." *Medical Anthropology Newsletter* 2 (5).

———— 1980b. "The Sounds of Silence in Nohya: A Preliminary Account of Sign Language Use by the Deaf in a Maya Community in Yucatan, Mexico." *Language Sciences* 2 (1): 144–173.

———— 1980c. "Culture and Deafness in a Maya Indian Village." *Psychiatry* 43: 359–370.

Sibscota, George. 1967. *The Deaf and Dumb Man's Discourse.* Menston, England: Scholar Press.

Siger, Lenard C. 1968. "Gestures, the Language of Signs and Human Communication" *American Annals of the Deaf* 113 (1): 11–28.

Silverman, S. R. 1970. "From Aristotle to Bell—and Beyond." In *Hearing and Deafness,* 3d ed., ed. Davis Hallowell and S. Richard Silverman. New York: Holt, Rinehart and Winston, pp. 375–382.

Simon, Anne W. 1973. *No Island Is an Island: The Ordeal of Martha's Vineyard.* Garden City, N.Y.: Doubleday.

Slatis, Herman M. 1958. "Comments on the Inheritance of Deaf Mutism in Northern Ireland." *Annals of Human Genetics* 22: 153–157.

Spuhler, J. N., and C. Kluckhohn. 1953. "Inbreeding Coefficients of Ramah Navaho Populations." *Human Biology* 25: 295–317.

Stevenson, A. C., and E. A. Cheeseman. 1956. "Hereditary Deaf Mutism with Particular Reference to Northern Ireland." *Annals of Human Genetics* 20: 177–207.

Stokoe, William C., Jr. 1960. *Sign Language Structure: An Outline of the Visual Communication Systems of the American Deaf.* Studies in Linguistics, occasional paper, no. 8. Buffalo: University of Buffalo Press.

——— 1972. *Semiotics and Human Sign Language.* The Hague: Mouton.

——— 1974. "The Classification and Description of Sign Languages." In *Current Trends in Linguistics,* ed. T. Sebeok. 12: 346-371. The Hague: Mouton.

——— 1980. "Sign Language Structure." *Annual Review of Anthropology* 9: 365–390.

Stokoe, William, and Robin Battison. 1975. "Sign Language, Mental Health and Satisfying Interaction." In *Needs of Deaf Adults and Youth,* Proceedings of the First National Symposium on Mental Health, ed. Mindel and Stien. New York: Grune and Stratton.

Stokoe, William, Dorothy Casterline, and Carl Croneberg. 1976. *A Dictionary of American Sign Language on Linguistic Principles,* new ed. Silver Spring, Md.: Linstock Press.

Sutter, Jean, and Tran-Ngoc Toan. 1957. "The Problem of the Structure of Isolates and of Their Evolution Among Human Populations." *Cold Spring Harbor Symposium in Quantitative Biology* 22: 379–383.

Swedlund, Alan C. 1972. "Observations on the Concept of Neighbourhood Knowledge and the Distribution of Marriage Distances." *Annals of Human Genetics* 35: 327–330.

Swett, William B. 1859. "Obituary of Nahum Brown, an Aged Deaf-Mute." *American Annals of the Deaf and Dumb* 6 (4): 236–240.

Tervoot, Bernard T. 1978. "Bilingual Interference." In *Sign Language of the Deaf,* ed. Schlesinger and Namir. New York: Academic Press.

Thaxter, Joseph. 1968. "The Hazards of Seafaring: Martha's Vineyard 1780–1827, from Joseph Thaxter's Records." *Dukes County Intelligencer,* November.

Trayser, Donald G. 1939. *Barnstable, Three Centuries of a Cape Cod Town.* Hyannis, Mass.: F. B. and F. P. Goss.

Trybus, Raymond J., and Michael A. Karchman. 1977. "School Achievement Scores of Hearing Impaired Children: National Data on Achievement Status and Growth Patterns." *American Annals of the Deaf* 122: 62–69.

Turner, W. W. 1847. "Causes of Deafness." *American Annals of the Deaf and Dumb* 1 (1): 25–32.

———— 1868. "Hereditary Deafness." *Proceedings of the First Conference of Principals of American Schools for the Deaf.* Washington, D.C., May 12– 16, p. 91.

United States Department of Commerce, Bureau of the Census. 1918. *Deaf-Mutes in the United States: Analysis of the Census of 1910 with Summary of State Laws Relative to the Deaf as of January 1, 1918.* Washington D.C.: Government Printing Office.

Vernon, McCay, and B. Markowsky. 1969. "Deafness and Minority Group Dynamics." *Deaf American* 21: 3–6.

Vineyard Gazette. 1922. "Alexander Graham Bell at Edgartown—Inventor Had Interesting Association with the Vineyard." August 24.

Washabaugh, William. 1980a. "The Organization and Use of Providence Island Sign Language." *Sign Language Studies* 26: 65–92.

———— 1980b. "The Manu-facturing of a Language." *Semiotica* 29 (1–2): 1– 37.

———— 1981. "The Deaf of Grand Cayman, British West Indies." *Sign Language Studies* 31: 117–134.

Washabaugh, William, James C. Woodward, and Susan Desantis. 1978. "Providence Island Sign Language: A Context-Dependent Language." *Anthropological Linguistics* 20 (3): 95–109.

Weld, Lewis. 1828. "An Address Delivered in the Capital in Washington City, Feb. 16th, 1828 at an Exhibition of Three of the Pupils of the Pennsylvania Institution for the Education of the Deaf and Dumb." Washington: Way and Gideon.

———— 1848. "The American Asylum." *American Annals of the Deaf and Dumb* 1 (2): 93–112.

Wilbur, R. B., and M. L. Jones. 1974. "Some Aspects of Bilingual/Bimodal Acquisition of Sign and English by Three Hearing Children of Deaf Parents." In *Proceedings of the Tenth Regional Meeting, Chicago Linguistics Society,* ed. R. Fox and A. Bruck. Chicago.

Wildervanck, L. S. 1957. "Consanguinity and Congenital Deaf Mutism in the Netherlands: Are the Parents of Deaf Children Detectable as Heterozygotes?" *Acta Genetica* 7: 244–248.

Williams, Job. 1891. "Hereditary Deafness—A Study." *Science* 17 (418): 76–77.

Wilson, Peter. 1974. *Oscar: An Inquiry into the Nature of Sanity.* New York: Random House, Vintage Books.

Winthrop, John. 1959. Winthrop's Journal. In *History of New England, 1630–1649,* ed. James Kendall Hosmer, vols. 1 and 2. New York: Barnes and Noble.

Withington, Charles Francis. 1885. *Consanguineous Marriages: Their Effect Upon Offspring.* Boston.

Woll, B., J. Kyle, and M. Deuchar. 1981. *Perspectives on British Sign Language and Deafness.* Guildford, England: Billing and Sons.

Wood, Philip H. N. 1980. *International Classification of Impairments, Disabilities and Handicaps: A Manual of Classification Relating to the Consequences of Disease.* Geneva: World Health Organization.

Woodward, James C. 1972. "Implications for Sociolinguistic Research among the Deaf." *Sign Language Studies* 1: 1–7.

———— 1973a. "Some Observations on Sociolinguistic Variation and American Sign Language." *Kansas Journal of Sociology* 9 (2): 191–199.

———— 1973b. "Some Characteristics of Pidgin Sign English." *Sign Language Studies* 3: 39–46.

———— 1974. "Implicational Variation in American Sign Language." *Sign Language Studies* 5: 20–30.

———— 1976. "Signs of Change: Historical Variation in American Sign Language." *Sign Language Studies* 10: 81–95.

———— 1978a. "Attitudes Toward Providence Island Sign Language." *Sign Language Studies* 18: 49–68.

———— 1978b. "Historical Bases of American Sign Language." In *Understanding Language Through Sign Language Research,* ed. P. Siple. New York: Academic Press.

———— 1980. "The Organization and Use of Providence Island Sign Language." *Sign Language Studies* 26: 65–92.

Woodward, James C., and Carol Erting. 1975. "Synchronic Variation and Historical Change in American Sign Language." *Language Sciences* 37: 9–12.

Woodward, James C., and H. Markowicz. 1975. "Some Handy New Ideas on Pidgins and Creoles: Pidgin Sign Languages." Paper presented at the International Conference on Pidgin and Creole Languages. Honolulu, Hawaii.

Index